Hal Elrod is a genius and his book *The Miracle Morning* has been magical in my life.

I have been in the *human potential/personal development movement* since 1973, when I did my first EST training and saw a whole new world of possibilities. Since then, I have studied religions, prayer, meditation, yoga, affirmation, visualization and NLP (neuro-linguistic programming). I've walked on fire, and explored other 'unconventional' philosophies, some 'too far out there' to mention.

What Hal has done with his acronym SAVERS is taken the 'best practices' – developed over centuries of human consciousness development – and condensed the 'best of the best' into a daily morning ritual. A ritual that is now part of my day.

'Many people do *one* of the SAVERS daily. For example, many people do the E, the *exercise* every morning. Others do S for *silence* or meditation, or S for *scribing*, journaling every morning. But until Hal packaged SAVERS, no one was doing all six ancient 'best practices' every morning.

The Miracle Morning is perfect for very busy, successful people. Going through SAVERS every morning is like pumping rocket fuel into my body, mind and spirit … *before* I start my day, every day.

As my rich dad often said, 'I can always make another dollar, but I cannot make another day'. If you want to maximize every day of your life, read *The Miracle Morning*.

Robert Kiyosaki, bestselling author, Rich Dad, Poor Dad

Every once in a while you read a book that changes the way you look at life, but it is so rare to find a book that changes the way you live your life. *The Miracle Morning* does both, and faster than you ever thought possible.

Tim Sanders, former Chief Solutions Officer at Yahoo!
NY Times *bestselling author,* The Likeability Factor

To read *The Miracle Morning* is to give yourself the gift of waking up each day to your full potential. It's time to stop putting off creating the life you want, and deserve, to live. Read this book and find out how.

Dr. Ivan Misner, CEO and Founder of BNI®

Hal Elrod is more than an inspiration. He has taken his incredible story and turned it into lessons that you can use to create your own miracles.

Jeffrey Gitomer, NY Times *bestselling author,*
The Sales Bible

The Miracle Morning is the ONE thing that can make immediate and profound changes in any – or every area of your life. If you want your life to improve NOW, I highly recommend reading this book immediately.

Rudy Ruettiger, the famous Notre Dame football player who inspired the hit Hollywood movie Rudy

I've always been a night owl so the idea of creating a morning routine was never an option and didn't appeal to me. Things were already going well with my current schedule, so why fix it if it's not broken? But I kept hearing about how valuable people's morning routines are to their success, their mood, and their lives. So, I made a commitment to give *The Miracle Morning* a shot. I've been doing it the last three weeks, and already I'm seeing massive changes in my focus, in my mood and in how much I'm able to get done.

Pat Flynn, author of Let's Go *and host of the #1 rated 'Smart Passive Income' podcast*

I never thought I would say this about a 'morning book', but *The Miracle Morning* CHANGED MY LIFE. Yes, you read that correctly. For years I've told myself 'I'm not a morning person' and for the most part, it was true. In fact, one of my WHYs for wanting to be an entrepreneur was my desire to sleep in. No alarm clock. No getting up at dark. I wanted to wake up when I wanted to wake up. When I started reading this, I was curious to see if it could break my strong narrative and my strong why. It did. After reading this book I actually started getting up at 4.00 am and hitting the gym. Yes, you read that right – 4 FREAKING AM. As a result, my days are far more productive and my physique is changing before my eyes. I never thought I could be one of these weirdos who get up at 4 am. Now I'm one of those weirdos. I do it five times a week, and mostly without an alarm clock.

MJ DeMarco, former CEO of Limos.com and #1 bestselling author, The Millionaire Fastlane

As a speaker, author, and business marketing consultant, I see the biggest thing holding people back from achieving the success they want is not that they don't know what to do; it's finding the time and motivation to do what they know. Hal Elrod has literally solved this problem. *The Miracle Morning* gives you the time and motivation you need to create the success you want, no matter how busy you are. I highly, highly recommend it.

James Malinchak, featured on ABC's hit TV show Secret Millionaire, *co-author of* Chicken Soup for the College Soul *and founder of www.MillionaireSpeakerSecrets.com*

At first I thought Hal had lost his mind – why on earth would anyone get up so early on a regular basis?!?! I was sceptical … until I tried it. When I implemented Hal's strategies I noticed an immediate difference in my personal and professional life. *The Miracle Morning* will show you how to take control of your life, regardless of your past. I highly recommend it.

Josh Shipp, TV host, author, and teen behaviour expert

Reading Hal's first book, *Taking Life Head On*, completely changed the way I live each day, and I've been waiting patiently for his next book. All I can say is that *The Miracle Morning* was definitely worth the wait! Hal gives us the blueprint for creating the success, happiness and prosperity that may have eluded us, and he's made it so simple that anyone can turn their life around – no matter what their circumstances.

Debra Poneman, co-author of Chicken Soup
for the American Idol® Soul *and founder of*
Yes to Success, Inc.

The Miracle Morning truly changed my life. It allowed me to start tapping into my full potential, which ultimately led me to a path of expanded consciousness that continues to reveal new opportunities and abilities.

Nick Conedera, film director, SHARP:
The World's Finest Movie

The Miracle Morning is the most paradigm-shifting book since The *4-Hour Workweek*. Hal lives and breathes the habits that he teaches, and this book will show you how to take your life and business to the next level.

Brad Weimert, CEO of Easy Pay Direct,
EasyPayDirect.com

If you are ready to leave mediocrity behind you and maximize your potential, read this book, plain and simple. *The Miracle Morning* gives you the key to unlock your personal power and tap into the abilities that allow ordinary people to become extraordinary.

Gail Lynne Goodwin, founder of InspireMeToday.com

The Miracle Morning is literally the ONE thing that changes EVERYTHING for people. I recommend it to all of my Game Changers coaching members, and I guarantee it will be a game changer for you.

Peter Voogd, #1 bestselling author, 6 Months to 6 Figures

The Miracle Morning

The Miracle Morning

The 6 Habits That Will Transform Your Life Before 8AM

HAL ELROD

JOHN
MURRAY
LEARNING

First published in Great Britain in 2016 by Hodder & Stoughton.
An Hachette UK Company.
This edition published in Great Britain in 2017 by John Murray Learning.
Copyright © Hal Elrod 2016

British Library Cataloguing in Publication Data: a catalogue record for this title is
available from the British Library.
Library of Congress Catalog Card Number: on file.

Trade Paperback: 978 1 47363 215 8
Paperback: 978 1 47366 894 2
eBook: 978 1 47363 216 5

50

The publisher has used its best endeavours to ensure that any website addresses
referred to in this book are correct and active at the time of going to press.
However, the publisher and the author have no responsibility for the websites and
can make no guarantee that a site will remain live or that the content will remain
relevant, decent or appropriate.

The publisher has made every effort to mark as such all words which it believes to
be trademarks. The publisher should also like to make it clear that the presence of
a word in the book, whether marked or unmarked, in no way affects its legal status
as a trademark.

Every reasonable effort has been made by the publisher to trace the copyright
holders of material in this book. Any errors or omissions should be notified in
writing to the publisher, who will endeavour to rectify the situation for any
reprints and future editions.

Typeset by Cenveo® Publisher Services.
Printed and bound in India by Manipal Technologies Limited, Manipal

MIX
Paper from
responsible sources
FSC
www.fsc.org   FSC™ C104740

Carmelite House
50 Victoria Embankment
London EC4Y 0DZ
www.hodder.co.uk

Also available
in ebook

This book is dedicated to the most important people in my life – my family. Mom, Dad, Hayley, my wife, Ursula, and our two children – Sophie and Halsten. I love you all more than I can put into words.
This book is in loving memory of my sister, Amery Kristine Elrod

The Miracle Morning *Mission*

Change one million lives, one morning at a time

In addition to donating a percentage of the royalties from each copy of *The Miracle Morning* to non-profit charities including the Front Row Foundation, thousands of copies of *The Miracle Morning* book are donated each year to organizations and individuals that are in desperate need of inspiration and transformation. Our mission is to get TMM in the hands of 1,000,000+ people so that we can literally change one million lives, one Miracle Morning at a time. Thank you so much for your support!

FrontRowFoundation.org

Contents

Miracle Morning success stories and results

Just read a few, to see what's possible for YOU ...

I am on day 79 of *The Miracle Morning*, and since I began, I have not missed a single day. Honestly, this is the FIRST time I've ever set out to do something and have actually stuck with it for more than just a couple of days or weeks! I now look forward to waking up every day. It's incredible, *The Miracle Morning* has completely changed my life.

Melanie Deppen, entrepreneur (Selinsgrove, PA)

Today is Day 60 for me! My Miracle Morning accomplishments so far:

- I have lost 20 pounds and 55 inches.
- I completely quit smoking.
- I have WAY more energy throughout the day.
- I'm happy all the time
- *The Miracle Morning* just keeps me pushing forward to become a better version of myself!

Dawn Pogue, sales rep (Lakefield, ON, Canada)

A few months ago, I decided to try *The Miracle Morning*. My life is changing so fast I cannot keep up! I'm such a better person because of this, and it's infectious. My business was struggling, but after I started *The Miracle Morning* I was amazed at how, just by working on myself every day, I was able to turn it all around.

Rob Leroy, senior account executive (Sacramento, CA)

After beginning *The Miracle Morning* in December, 2009, as a college student at UC Davis, I noticed profound changes immediately. I quickly began to achieve long-desired goals more easily than I would have ever expected. I lost weight, found a new love, attained my best grades ever, and even created multiple streams of income – all in less than two months! Now, years later, *The Miracle Morning* is still an integral part of my daily life.

Natanya Green, yoga instructor (Sacramento, CA)

Every time I do *The Miracle Morning*, not only do I feel amazing, but I've actually lost 25 pounds as a result. I have never been happier, healthier, and more productive! I now get more done in a day than I ever thought to be possible in the past. Oh, and did I mention that I've already lost 25 pounds?

William Hougen, district manager (Gresham, OR)

I've been using *The Miracle Morning* for ten months. Since then, my income has more than doubled, I am in the best shape of my life, and never have I been more present to creating better memories with family and friends than I have since after I started. Needless to say, I am a HUGE fan!

Mike McDermott, region sales manager (Davis, CA)

When I first heard about *The Miracle Morning*, I thought to myself, 'this is so crazy that it just might work!' I am a college student taking 19 units and working full time, so that left me with zero time to work on my goals. Before I learned *The Miracle Morning*, I used to wake up between 7 and 9 am every day – because I had to get ready for class – but now I consistently wake up at 5 am. I am learning and growing so much through daily personal development, and I am LOVING *The Miracle Morning*!

Michael Reeves, college student (Walnut Creek, CA)

I don't really know what to say, other than that my days are 100 times better when I do *The Miracle Morning*.

Josh Thielbar, business development consultant (Boise, ID)

I'm on my 83rd consecutive day of *The Miracle Morning* and just wish I had known about it sooner. It is amazing how much clarity I now have throughout the day. I am able to focus on my work and other tasks each day with so much more energy and enthusiasm. Thanks to *The Miracle Morning*, I am experiencing a richer more abundant way of living – both in my personal and professional life.

Ray Ciafardini, district manager (Baltimore, MD)

After implementing *The Miracle Morning* for only three weeks, I was able to quit taking medication for energy that I've been taking for over three years! *The Miracle Morning* has changed my life in many ways, and I'm sure it will change yours.

Sarah Geyer, college student (Minneapolis, MN)

The Miracle Morning started me on a whole new chapter in my life. It can do the same for you. Thank you, Hal!

Andrew Barksdale, entrepreneur (Vienna, VA)

The Miracle Morning makes every day feel like Christmas. Literally. Now I even do it on the weekends.

Joseph Diosana, realtor (Houston, TX)

A note to YOU, the reader

No matter where you are in your life right now — whether you're currently at the top of your game, succeeding at the highest level, or if you're in the midst of adversity and struggling to find your way — there is at least one thing I know we have in common (probably a lot more than *one*, but at least one that I know for sure): we both want to improve our lives, and ourselves. This is not to suggest that there is anything *wrong* with us, or our lives, but as human beings we were born with the innate desire and drive to continuously grow and improve. I believe it's within all of us. Yet, most of us wake up each day, and life pretty much stays the same.

As an author, keynote speaker, and life/business success coach, my work is focused on helping people take every area of their lives to new levels of success and fulfilment, as fast as possible. As a dedicated student of human potential and personal development, I can say with absolute certainty that *The Miracle Morning* is the most practical, results-oriented, and effective method I have ever encountered for improving any — or *every* area of your life, and doing so faster than you probably even believe is possible.

For achievers and top performers, *The Miracle Morning* can be an absolute game-changer, allowing you to attain that elusive next level and take your personal and professional success far beyond what you've achieved in the past. While this can include increasing your income or growing your business, sales and revenue, it's often more about discovering new ways to experience deeper levels of fulfilment and balance in areas of your life that you may have neglected. This can mean making significant improvements with your health, happiness, relationships, finances, spirituality, or any other areas that are at the top of your list.

For those who are in the midst of adversity or enduring times of struggle – be it mental, emotional, physical, financial, relational or other – *The Miracle Morning* has proven time and time again to be the one thing that can empower anyone to overcome seemingly insurmountable challenges, make major breakthroughs, and turn their circumstances around, often in a very short period of time.

Whether you want to make significant improvements in just a few key areas, or you are ready for a major overhaul that will radically transform your entire life – so your current circumstances will soon become only a memory of what was – you've picked up the right book. You are about to begin a miraculous journey, using a simple, but revolutionary process that is guaranteed to transform any area of your life... all before 8.00 am.

I know, I know – these are big promises to make. But *The Miracle Morning* has already generated measurable results for (literally) tens of thousands of people around the world (myself included), and it can absolutely be the one thing that takes you to where you want to be. I consider it a great honour to share this with you now, and I have done everything in my power to ensure that this book will truly be a life-changing investment of your time, energy and attention. Thank you for allowing me to be a part of your life; our miraculous journey together is about to begin.

With love and gratitude,

Hal

A special invitation

The Miracle Morning *Community*

Fans and readers of *The Miracle Morning* make up an extraordinary tribe of like-minded individuals, who wake up each day *on purpose*, dedicated to fulfilling the unlimited potential that is within each of us. As creator of *The Miracle Morning*, I felt it was my responsibility to create an online community where readers and fans could go to connect, get encouragement, share best practices, support one another, discuss the book, post videos, find an accountability partner, and even swap smoothie recipes and exercise routines.

I honestly had no idea that *The Miracle Morning* Community would become one of the most positive, inspired, supportive and accountable online communities that I have ever seen, but it has. I'm truly blown away by the calibre of our members.

Just go to www.MiracleMorning.com/resources and request to join *The Miracle Morning* Community on Facebook. Here you'll be able to connect with like-minded individuals who are already practising *The Miracle Morning* – many of whom have been doing it for years – to get additional support and accelerate your success.

I'll be moderating the community and checking in regularly. I look forward to seeing you there! If you'd like to connect with me personally on social media, follow @HalElrod on Twitter and www.Facebook.com/YoPalHal on Facebook. Please feel free to send me a direct message, leave a comment, or ask me a question. I do my best to answer every single one, so let's connect soon!

There are only two ways to live your life. One is as though nothing is a miracle. The other is as though everything is a miracle.

Albert Einstein

Miracles do not happen in contradiction with nature, but in contradiction with what we know about nature.

Saint Augustine

Life begins each morning.

Joel Olsteen

Introduction

My story, and why yours is the one that matters

3 December 1999. Life was good. No, it was *great*. At 20 years old, my first year of college was behind me. I had spent the last 18 months becoming one of the top-producing sales reps for a $200- million marketing company, breaking company records and earning more money than I had ever imagined I would be at that age. I was in love with my girlfriend, had a supportive family, and the best friends a guy could ask for. I was truly blessed.

You might say I was on top of the world. There was no way I could have known that this was the night my world would end.

11.32 pm. Driving 70 mph southbound on Highway 99.

We'd left the restaurant, and our friends, behind. It was just the two of us now. My girlfriend, tired from the evening's events, was dozing in the passenger seat. Not me. I was wide-awake – eyes glued to the road in front, waving my finger in the air like a baton as I quietly conducted the melodies of Tchaikovsky.

Still in a state of euphoria from the night's events, sleep was the furthest thing from my mind. Rocketing down the freeway at 70 miles per hour in my brand new white Ford Mustang, I was only two hours removed from giving the best speech of my life. I had received my first standing ovation, and I was elated. In fact, I desperately wanted to shout out my feelings of gratitude to anyone that would listen, but my girlfriend was asleep, so she was no use. I considered calling my parents, but it was late; they might already be in bed. Should've called. But I simply had no way of knowing that moment would be my last opportunity to speak to my parents – or anyone – for quite some time.

An unimaginable reality

No, I don't recall seeing the headlights of a massive Chevrolet truck coming directly at me. But they were. In an instant of perverse fate, the full-size Chevy pick-up, travelling at an estimated 80 mph, smashed head on into my undersized, and under-matched Ford Mustang. The following seconds played out in slow motion, Tchaikovsky's commanding melodies orchestrating our wicked dance.

The metal frames of our two vehicles collided – screaming and screeching as they twisted and broke. The Mustang's airbags exploded with enough force to render us unconscious. My brain, still travelling at 70 mph, smashed into the front of my skull, destroying much of the vital brain tissue that made up my frontal lobe.

Upon impact, the tail-end of my Mustang was shoved into the lane on my right, making my driver's-side door an unavoidable target for the car behind me. A Saturn Sedan, driven by a 16-year-old, crashed into my door at 70 mph. The door collapsed into the left side of my body. The frame of the metal roof caved in on my head, slicing open my skull and nearly severing my left ear. The bones of my left eye socket were crushed, leaving my left eyeball dangerously unsupported. My left arm broke, severing the radial nerve in my forearm and shattering my elbow, while my fractured humerus bone pierced the skin behind my bicep.

My pelvis was given the impossible task of separating the Saturn's front end from my car's centre console, and failed. It fractured in three separate places. Finally, my femur – the largest bone in the human body – snapped in half, and one end speared through the skin of my thigh and tore a hole in my black dress slacks.

Blood was everywhere. My body was destroyed. My brain was permanently damaged.

Unable to withstand the immense physical pain, my body shut down, my blood pressure dropped, and everything went black as I plunged into a coma.

You only live ... twice?

What happened next was nothing short of incredible – what many have called a *miracle*.

The emergency rescue teams arrived, and, using the jaws of life, firefighters cut my bloody body from the wreckage. When they did, I bled out. My heart stopped beating. I stopped breathing.

Clinically, I was dead.

The paramedics immediately put me on the rescue helicopter and worked determinedly to save my life. Six minutes later, they succeeded. My heart started to beat again. I breathed clean oxygen. Thankfully, I was alive.

I spent six days in a coma, and woke to the news that I might never walk again. After seven challenging weeks of recovery and rehabilitation in the hospital, learning to walk all over again, I was released to my parents' care – back into the real world. With 11 fractured bones, permanent brain damage, and a now ex-girlfriend who broke up with me in the hospital, life as I knew it, would never be the same. Believe it or not, this would turn out to be a good thing.

While coming to grips with my new reality wasn't easy, and at times – I couldn't help but wonder *why did this happen to me?* – I had to take responsibility for getting my life back. Instead of complaining about how things *should* be, I embraced how things were. I stopped putting energy into *wishing* my life were any different — into wishing *bad things* didn't happen to me — and instead focused 100% on making the best of what I had. Since I couldn't change the past, I focused on moving forward. I dedicated my life to fulfilling my potential and achieving my dreams so I could discover how to empower others to do the same.

And, as a result of choosing to be genuinely *grateful* for all that I had, unconditionally *accepting* of all that I didn't, and accepting total responsibility for *creating* all that I wanted, this potentially devastating car accident ultimately became one of the best things that ever happened to me. Hinging on my belief that everything happens for a reason — but that it is *our responsibility to choose the most empowering reasons* for the challenges, events and circumstances of our lives — I used my accident to fuel a triumphant comeback.

2000. A year that begins with me lying in a hospital bed — broken, but not defeated — ends quite differently. Despite not having a car, even less of a short-term memory, equipped with every excuse in the world to sit at home and feel sorry for myself, I returned to my sales position at Cutco. I had the best year in my career, and finished #6 in the company (amongst over 60,000 active sales reps). All this, while still recovering — physically, mentally, emotionally, and financially — from my wreck.

2001. Having learned some invaluable life lessons from my experience, it was time to turn my adversity into inspiration and empowerment for others. I started speaking and sharing my story at high schools and colleges. The responses from students and faculty were overwhelmingly positive, and I embarked on a mission to impact youth.

2002. My good friend, Jon Berghoff, encouraged me to write a book about my accident, to further inspire others. So, I started writing. As quickly as I started, I stopped. I'm no *writer*. Essays in high school were challenging enough, let alone a book. After repeated attempts that always ended with me staring at my computer screen, frustrated, it didn't look like a book was on the cards. I did, however, finish in Cutco's Top 10 for the second year in a row.

2004. To try my hand at management, I accepted the position as Sales Manager for the Sacramento Cutco office. Our team went on to finish #1 in the company and break the all-time annual record. That autumn, I also reached my highest personal sales milestone and was inducted into the company's hall of fame. Feeling that I'd accomplished everything I wanted to accomplish with Cutco, it was time to pursue my dream of becoming a professional keynote/motivational speaker. I might even write that book that had been swimming around in my head the last couple of years. I also met Ursula. We were inseparable and I had this feeling that she could be the one.

February 2005. Sitting in the audience at what I intended to be my last Cutco conference, I came to a painful realization: *I have never fulfilled my potential.* Ouch. Sure, I'd won some awards and broken some sales records, but watching from my seat as the two top performers collect the highest annual award that Cutco offered – the coveted *Rolex* – I realized that I'd never fully committed, at least not for an entire year. I wouldn't be able to live with myself if I left the company before fulfilling my potential. I had to give it one more year, but this time I had to give it my all.

2005. Despite the late start to the year, I set a goal to nearly double my best sales year ever. I was terrified, but committed. I also concluded that I had an obligation to write that book and share my story with the world. I worked 365 days straight, selling and writing, with a level of discipline which eluded me the first 25 years of my life. I was fuelled by passion to do what I had never done before: to venture from my painfully comfortable realm of mediocrity – from which I operated my entire life – into the space of being extraordinary. By the year's end, I reached both of my goals, more than doubling my previous best sales year and completing my first book. It's official: anything is possible when you are committed.

Spring 2006. My first book, *Taking Life Head On: How to Love the Life You Have While You Create the Life of Your Dreams* hit #7 on the Amazon bestseller list. Then, the unthinkable happened. My publisher fled the country with 100% of my bestselling royalties and was never heard from again. My parents were devastated; I was not. If there's one thing that I've learned from my car accident, it's that there is no point in dwelling on or feeling bad about the aspects of our lives that we can't change. So, I didn't. I've also learned that, by focusing on what we can learn from our challenges and how we use them to add value to the lives of others, we can turn any adversity into an advantage. So, I did.

2006. Without almost zero knowledge of what the profession entails, I accidentally became a life and business success coach when a forty-something financial advisor asked me if I would coach him. I agreed. I ended up loving it. My first client saw measurable results in his life and business, and I was passionate about helping others, as their coach. At just 26, the odds of me succeeding as a professional coach were probably slim to none, but it's so in line with my purpose in life, I went for it anyway. My coaching business took off, and I went on to coach hundreds of entrepreneurs, salespeople, and business owners.

Shortly after, I gave my first *paid* speech when I was hired by the Boys and Girls Clubs of America to be the featured keynote speaker at their national conference. Although I'd been speaking to large business audiences made up of primarily salespeople, managers and executives, since 1998, I decided that with my spiky hair, (somewhat) youthful appearance, and the nickname 'Yo Pal Hal', impacting youth was the way to go. I started speaking and sharing my story at local high schools and colleges.

2007. The year my life fell apart. The United States economy crashed. Overnight, my income was cut in half. My clients couldn't afford coaching. I couldn't pay my bills, including my house payment. I was $425,000 in debt, and devastated. Mentally, physically, emotionally, and financially – I hit rock bottom. Never in my life have I felt so hopeless, overwhelmed, and depressed. At a loss for how to fix my life yet again, I desperately sought answers to insurmountable problems. I read self-help books, attended seminars, even hired a coach – but nothing worked.

2008. The year my life began to turn around. I finally confessed to a close friend how bad things had gotten (which I had successfully kept a secret up until this point). His question: *Are you exercising?* My answer: *I can barely get out of bed in the morning – so, no.*

Start running he said. *It'll help you feel better and think clearer.* Ugh, I hated running. I was desperate, though, so I took his advice and went for a run. The realizations I had on this run became a turning point in my life (details in Chapter 2), and I was inspired to create a daily personal development routine that I hoped would enable me to develop into the person I needed to be to solve my problems and turn my life around. Incredibly, it worked. Virtually every area of my life transformed so fast I called it my 'Miracle Morning'.

Autumn 2008. I continued developing *my* Miracle Morning, experimenting with various personal development practices and sleep schedules, and researching how much sleep we really need. My findings completely shattered the paradigms and perceptions held true by most people, including me. Loving the results, I shared it with my coaching clients, who loved it just as much. They told their friends, family, and co-workers about it. Unexpectedly, I began seeing people I'd never met posting on Facebook and Twitter about *their* Miracle Mornings (more on that later).

2009. Arguably my best year yet! I married the woman of my dreams. We got pregnant and gave birth to our daughter (can I say 'we' or is that more of a 'she' thing?) My coaching business was thriving; I had a waiting list for clients. My speaking career took off. I was giving talks and keynote messages at high schools, colleges, and corporate and non-profit conferences. *The Miracle Morning* spread like wildfire. I got emails every day from people telling me it was changing their life. I knew it was my responsibility to share it with the world, and that writing a book was the best way to do that. Slowly, I began to write again. Make no mistake, I'm still no writer — but I am committed. As my good friend Romacio Fulcher always says, 'There is *always* a way... when you're committed.'

2012. The book you hold in your hands, the one I'd dedicated over three years of my life to writing, *The Miracle Morning: The Not-So-Obvious Secret Guaranteed To Transform Your Life... (Before 8AM)* was finally published. I was blown away when it quickly became not only a #1 Amazon bestseller, but in its first year of publication, became one of the highest rated books in the history of Amazon (currently with over 500 reviews, averaging 4.7 out of 5 stars). More important is what the reviews actually said. People's lives were being changed. And it works for *all* types of people — from stay-at-home moms to CEOs, *The Miracle Morning* gives people the ability to improve any — or literally *every* area of their lives.

Taking your life head on

I share my story with you to offer evidence of what can be overcome and achieved, no matter where you are in your life right now, or how difficult your challenges may be. If I could go from being found dead, told I would never walk again, going broke and feeling so depressed that I didn't want to get out of bed in the morning to creating the life I've always wanted, then there are no legitimate excuses for you not to overcome any limitations that have held you back from achieving everything you want for your life. None. Zip. Nada.

I believe it is crucial for us to embrace the perspective that anything another person has overcome or accomplished is simply evidence that anything – and I mean *anything* – we need to overcome or want to accomplish is possible for us, no matter what our past or current circumstances. It begins with accepting total responsibility for every aspect of your life and refusing to blame anyone else. The degree to which you accept responsibility for *everything* in your life is precisely the degree of personal power you have to change or create *anything* in your life.

It is important to understand that responsibility is not the same as blame. While *blame determines who is at fault for something, responsibility determines who is committed to improving things*. Thinking back to my accident, while the drunk driver was at fault for the crash, I was responsible for improving *my* life – for making my circumstances what I wanted them to be. It really doesn't matter who is at fault – all that matters is that you and I are committed to leaving the past in the past and making our lives *exactly* the way we want them to be, starting today.

It's your time, this is YOUR story

Know that wherever you are in your life right now is both temporary, and exactly where you are supposed to be. You have arrived at this moment to learn what you must learn, so you can become the person you need to be to create the life you truly want. Even when life is difficult or challenging – *especially* when life is difficult or challenging – the present is always an opportunity for us to learn, grow, and become better than we've ever been before.

You are in the process of writing your life story, and no good story is without a hero or heroine overcoming their fair share of challenges. In fact, the bigger the challenges, the better the story. Since there are no restrictions and no limits to where your story goes from here, what do you want the next page to say?

The good news is that you have the ability to change – or create – anything in your life, starting right now. I'm not saying you won't have to work for it, but you can quickly and easily attract and create anything you want for your life by developing into the person who is capable of doing so. That's what this book is about – helping you become the person you need to be to create everything you have ever wanted for your life. There are no limits.

Grab a pen

Before you read any further, please grab a pen or pencil so you can write in this book. As you read, mark anything that stands out which you may want to come back to later. Underline, circle, highlight, fold the corners of pages and take notes in the margins so you can come back and quickly recall the most important lessons, ideas, and strategies.

Personally, I used to struggle with this, because I am a bit of an obsessive-compulsive perfectionist, and anal about keeping my things looking clean and neat. Then I realized that I needed to get over it, because the purpose of a book like this is not for it to remain untouched, but rather to maximize the value we extract from it. Now, I mark up all of my books so I can revisit them anytime and quickly recapture all of the key benefits, without having to read the entire book again.

Okay, with your pen in hand, let's get started! The next chapter *of your life* is about to begin…

1
It's time to wake up to your FULL potential

Life's too short' is repeated often enough to be a cliché, but this time it's true. You don't have enough time to be both unhappy and mediocre. It's not just pointless; it's painful.

Seth Godin

You've got to wake up every morning with determination if you're going to go to bed with satisfaction.

George Lorimer

Why is it that when a baby is born, we often refer to them as 'the miracle of life', but then go on to accept mediocrity for our own lives? Where along the way did we lose sight of the miracle that *we* are living?

When you were born, everyone assured you that you could do, have, and be anything you wanted when you grew up. So, now that you've grown up, are you doing, having, and being anything and everything you've ever wanted? Or somewhere along the way, did you redefine 'anything and everything' to include settling for less than you truly want?

I recently read an alarming statistic: The average American is 20 lb overweight, $10,000 in debt, slightly depressed, dislikes his or her job, and has less than one close friend. Even if only a fraction of this statistic is true, Americans need some serious waking up.

What about you? Are you maximizing your potential and creating the levels of success that you truly want – in *every* area of your life? Or are there areas of your life where you're settling for less than you really want? Are you settling for less than you're capable of, and then justifying that it's okay? Or are you ready to stop settling, so you can start living your best life – you know, the life of your dreams?

Creating your 'Level 10' life

One of my favourite sentiments ever shared by Oprah was when she said, 'The biggest adventure you can ever take is to live the life of your dreams.' I couldn't agree more. Sadly, so few people ever come close to living the life of their dreams that the phrase itself has become cliché. Most people resign themselves to a life of mediocrity, passively accepting whatever life gives them. Even achievers, who are highly successful in one area, such as business, tend to settle for mediocrity in another area, such as their health or relationships. As bestselling author,

Seth Godin so eloquently put it, 'Is there a difference between average and mediocre? Not so much.'

There is nothing that says you have to settle for less than you truly want in *any* area, just because most people do. Even if *most people* includes your friends, family, and colleagues. You can become one of the few people that actually achieve extraordinary success in EVERY area of your life, simultaneously. Happiness. Health. Money. Freedom. Success. Love. You really can have it all.

If we're measuring success, satisfaction, and fulfillment in any area of our lives on a scale of one to ten, we *all* want Level 10, right? I've never met anyone who said, 'Nah, I just want Level 7 health. I don't want to be too healthy and have too much energy.' Or, 'You know, I'm really okay with a Level 5 relationship. I don't really mind fighting with my significant other, *not* having my needs met, and I definitely don't want us to be one of those couples who are *so* happy that we annoy other couples.'

What you're about to find out is that achieving Level 10 success in every area is not only possible, it's simple. It's simply dedicating purposeful time each day to become a Level 10 person that is capable of creating, attracting, achieving, and sustaining Level 10 success in every area.

What if I told you that it all starts with how you wake up in the morning, and that there are small, simple steps you can start taking today that will enable you to become the person you need to be to create the levels of success you truly want and deserve – in *every* area of your life? Would you get excited? Would you even believe me? Some won't. Too many people have been jaded. They've tried everything under the sun to fix their lives, their relationships, and they're still not where they want to be. I understand. I've been there. Then, over time, I learned a few things that changed everything. I'm offering you my hand and inviting you to the other side, the side where life is not only good, it's extraordinary in a way we have only imagined it could be.

4

This book builds three imperative arguments:

1 You are just as worthy, deserving, and capable of creating and sustaining extraordinary health, wealth, happiness, love, and success in your life, as any other person on earth. It is absolutely crucial – not only for the quality of your life, but for the impact you make on your family, friends, clients, co-workers, children, community, and anyone whose life you touch – that you start living in alignment with that truth.

2 In order for you to stop settling for less than you deserve – in any area of your life – and to create the levels of personal, professional, and financial success you desire, you must first dedicate time each day to becoming the person you need to be, one who is qualified and capable of consistently attracting, creating, and sustaining the levels of success you want.

3 How you wake up each day and your morning routine (or lack thereof) dramatically affects your levels of success in every single area of your life. Focused, productive, successful mornings generate focused, productive, successful days – which inevitably create a successful life – in the same way that unfocused, unproductive, and mediocre mornings generate unfocused, unproductive, and mediocre days, and ultimately a mediocre quality of life. By simply changing the way you wake up in the morning, you can transform any area of your life, faster than you ever thought possible.

But Hal, I am NOT a 'morning person'

What if you've already tried waking up earlier, and it hasn't worked?

'I'm not a morning person,' you say.

'I'm a night owl.'

'There's not enough time in the day.' 'Besides, I need *more* sleep, not less!'

That was all true for me, too, before *The Miracle Morning*. If you read the opening page of this book, you'll see that it was also true for top achievers (and now Miracle Morning practitioners), Pat Flynn and MJ DeMarco. Regardless of your past experiences – even if you've had trouble waking up and getting going in the morning for your entire life – things are about to change.

The Miracle Morning has been proven to work for *everyone's* lifestyle (you'll see how you can make it work for YOU in Chapter 8). These newbie 'early risers' – from entrepreneurs, salespeople, and CEOs, to teachers, real estate agents, stay-at-home moms, high school and college students, and everyone in between – have been so excited about the profound changes they've experienced that many are even posting videos about their results on YouTube, and then sharing them with their friends on Facebook and Twitter.

Just read a few of the success stories in the opening pages of this book, and you will see the profound effects. You'll see real-life results, such as, 'My life is changing so fast, I can't keep up … My business was struggling, but after I started *The Miracle Morning*, I was amazed at how, just by working on myself every day, I was able to turn it all around.'

And, 'I'm on day 79 of *The Miracle Morning* and haven't missed a single day. This is the FIRST time I've ever set out to do something and actually stuck with it longer than a few days or weeks.'

Even, 'Since starting *The Miracle Morning*, ten months ago, my income has more than doubled and I am in the best shape of my life.'

And one of my favourites: 'I've lost 25 lb using *The Miracle Morning*!'" Increased income, improved quality of life, more discipline, less stress, and even weight loss – it's all available to you.

In the next chapter, I'm going to walk you through exactly how I used *The Miracle Morning* to go from my lowest point – a failing business, drowning in $425,000 of personal debt, deeply depressed, and physically in the worst shape of my life – to building multiple successful businesses, more than doubling my income, paying off 100% of my debt, and achieving my dreams of becoming an international keynote speaker, having my story featured in the bestselling *Chicken Soup for the Soul* book series, being interviewed on radio and TV shows across the country, and performing at my mental and physical peak by completing a 52-mile ultra-marathon – all in less than 12 months. You'll also discover some 'not-so-obvious secrets' that will make your success virtually guaranteed.

The Miracle Morning is not only simple, it's extremely enjoyable, and something you'll soon be able to do effortlessly, for the rest of your life. And, while you can still sleep in any time you want, you might be surprised to find you no longer want to. I can't tell you how many people have told me that they now wake up early – even on the weekends – simply because they feel better and get more done when they do. Imagine that.

Time and time again, practitioners of *The Miracle Morning* have compared doing it each day to the feeling they had as a kid, waking up on Christmas morning. It feels that good! If you don't celebrate Christmas, think back to a time where you were excited to wake up – maybe your first day of school, your birthday, or to go on holiday. Imagine how great it will be to start every single day like that.

Here are some of the most common, yet profound benefits you can expect to gain:

- Wake up every day with more energy, and empowered with the structure and strategy to start maximizing your potential.
- Lower your stress.
- Gain the clarity to quickly overcome any challenge, adversity or limiting beliefs that have been holding you back.
- Improve your overall health, lose weight (if desired), and get in the best physical shape of your life.
- Increase your productivity and enhance your ability to maintain laser focus on your top priorities.
- Experience more gratitude and less worry.
- Significantly increase your ability to earn and attract more monetary wealth.
- Uncover and begin living your life's purpose.
- Stop settling for less than you truly desire and deserve (in any area of your life) and start living in alignment with your vision for the most extraordinary life you can imagine.
- I realize that I'm making a lot of bold claims here, and it might come across as 'hype' or overpromising – *a little too good to be true*, right? But I assure you there is no hyperbole here. *The Miracle Morning* is going to give you uninterrupted time each day to become the person you need to be to improve any area of your life.

I'm also going to give you the *Life S.A.V.E.R.S.* – six powerful, proven practices which combine to make up *The Miracle Morning* and are guaranteed to save you from missing out on the extraordinary life you deserve to live – the one which, statistically, 95% of our society will sadly never experience (more on that in Chapter 3). With your help, I believe we can change that statistic.

Finally, you'll be ready to embark on *The Miracle Morning 30-Day Life Transformation Challenge* which will develop the mindset and cement the habits you'll need to easily and continuously attract, create, and sustain the levels of success you desire and deserve, in *every* area of your life. Never forget that *who you are becoming* is the single most important determining factor in your quality of life, now and for your future.

Whether you currently consider yourself to be a 'morning person' or not, you're going to learn how to make waking up every day easier than it's ever been before. Then, by taking advantage of the undeniable relationship between early rising and extraordinary success, you'll find that how you spend the first hour of your day becomes the key to unlocking your full potential and creating the levels of success you desire. You'll quickly see that when you change the way you wake up in the morning, you change your entire life.

2

The Miracle Morning origins:
born out of desperation

Desperation is the raw material of drastic change. Only those
who can leave behind everything they have ever believed in, can
hope to escape.

William S. Burroughs

To make profound changes in your life, you need either
inspiration or desperation.

Anthony Robbins

I've been fortunate to hit what you might call 'rock bottom' twice in my relatively short life. I say *fortunate* because it was the growth I experienced and the lessons I learned – during the most challenging times in my life – that have enabled me to become the person I've needed to be, to create the life that I've always wanted. I am grateful to use not only my successes, but also my failures, to help others in a way that can empower them to overcome their own limitations and achieve more than they ever thought possible.

My first rock bottom: dead at the scene

As you know, my first rock bottom was almost my last when, at age 20, I was hit head on by a drunk driver and died at the scene of the accident. (I wrote in detail about how I bounced back from my seemingly insurmountable adversity, as well as the eight lessons I learned that will immediately improve the quality of your life, in my first book, *Taking Life Head On: How To Love the Life You Have While You Create the Life of Your Dreams*.)

My second rock bottom: deep in debt and deeply depressed

My second plunge into the depths of despair was more difficult than dying in a car accident was.

It was 2008. The United States economy was in the midst of the worst recession since the infamous Great Depression of the 1930s. In the years after surviving my car accident, despite bouncing back to build a hall-of-fame sales career, launch a six-figure success coaching business, and write a bestselling book, I was again challenged. This time it was a complete mental, emotional, and financial breakdown.

Seemingly overnight, the successful enterprises I had built were no longer profitable. Over half of my monthly income disappeared. I was suddenly unable to pay my bills. I had just bought my first home. I was engaged to be married, and we were planning our first child. Buried in debt, behind on my mortgage, for the first time in my life, I became severely depressed.

I was at the lowest point in my life. Could things have been worse? Probably. But was this the worst they had ever been for me? Absolutely. I had hit *my* rock bottom.

Why debt was worse than death

If you were to ask me which was more difficult, my car accident or my financial struggles, I wouldn't hesitate to tell you it was the latter, by far. Most people would assume that being hit head on by a drunk driver, breaking 11 bones, suffering permanent brain damage, dying for six minutes, and waking from a coma to face the news that you may never walk again would be hard to top. It's a fair assumption that the physical, mental, and emotional pain from such a horrific wreck would be the lowest point in any person's life. However, this wasn't the case for me.

You see, after my car accident, I had people taking care of me. In the hospital, my family never left my side. I was constantly surrounded by visitors – friends and family coming by daily to check on me and shower me with love and support. I had an incredible staff of doctors and nurses overseeing every step of my care and recovery. My food was prepared and delivered to me. I didn't even have the everyday stresses of having to work and pay the bills. Life in the hospital was easy.

That wasn't the case the second time around. Nobody felt sorry for me. I didn't have any visitors. There was no one there to oversee my care and recovery. Nobody brought me any food. I was on my own this time. People had their own problems to deal with.

A domino effect led to struggles in every area of my life. Physically, mentally, emotionally, and financially – you name it – I was a mess.

I had so much fear and uncertainty that the only comfort I found each day was my own bed. As pathetic as it may sound, what got me through each day was the peace of mind from knowing I could eventually crawl into bed and temporarily escape my problems. Thoughts of suicide circled my mind daily, although I don't know that I would have ever followed through with it. Just knowing how much taking my own life would have devastated my mom and dad was enough for me to suck it up and move forward. Deep down, I knew that no matter how bad life gets, there is *always* a way to turn it around. But the thoughts were still there. I just didn't see a solution to my financial crisis. I couldn't think of anything else that would put an end to my emotional pain.

The morning that turned my life around

Then, in a single morning, everything changed. I woke up feeling depressed, as I had been for weeks, but this morning I *did* something different. I took a friend's advice and went on a run, to clear my head. Now, make no mistake, I was *not* a runner. In fact, running for the sake of running was one of the only things I can honestly say that I despised. However, my good friend, Jon Berghoff, told me that whenever he was feeling stressed or overwhelmed, going for a run enabled him to think more clearly, lifted his spirits, and helped him come up with solutions to his problems.

I told Jon, 'I hate running'. Without hesitation, he responded, 'What do you hate worse, running ... or your current life situation?' I was desperate. I had nothing to lose. I decided to go for a run.

That morning, I laced up my Nike Air Jordan® basketball shoes (I told you I wasn't a runner), grabbed my iPod so I could listen to something positive, and headed out the front door of my soon-to-be bank-owned home. I had no idea that, on that run, I would have one of the most powerful, profound, life-changing breakthroughs, which would immediately begin to change the course of my entire life.

Listening to a personal development audio from Jim Rohn, he said something that, although I had heard before, I never really *got it.* You know how sometimes you hear something over and over again without actually implementing it, but then one day it finally clicks for you? It just takes you being in the right state of mind to really *get it?* Well, that morning I was in the right state of mind – a state of desperation – and I got it. When I heard Jim proclaim with certainty, 'Your level of success, will rarely exceed your level of personal development, because success is something you attract by the person you become,' I stopped in my tracks. This one philosophy was going to change my entire life.

The success parallel

All of a sudden, it hit me! It was like a tidal wave of reality that came crashing down, and I became present to the fact that I had not been developing myself into the person I needed to be, to attract, create, and sustain the level of success that I wanted. On a scale of one to ten, I wanted Level 10 success, but my level of personal development was at about a 2 – maybe a 3 or a 4 on a good day.

I realized this is the problem for all of us. We all want Level 10 success, in every area of our lives – health, happiness, finances, relationships, career, spirituality, you name it – but if our levels of personal development (knowledge, experience, mindset, beliefs, etc.) in any given area are not at a Level 10, then life is always going to be a struggle.

Our outer world will always be a reflection of our inner world. Our level of success is always going to parallel our level of personal development. Until we dedicate time each day to developing ourselves into the person we need to be to create the life we want, success is always going to be a struggle to attain.

I ran straight home. I was ready to change my life.

Our first challenge: finding time

I knew that the solution to all of my problems was that I had to commit to making personal development a priority in my daily life. This was the missing link that would enable me to become the person I needed to be able to consistently attract, create, and sustain the levels of success that I wanted. Simple enough.

However, my main challenge was the same as anyone's: *finding time*. I was so busy just trying to survive my life and pay my bills, that the idea of finding 'extra' time for my personal development seemed almost impossible. Maybe you can relate?

I love what bestselling author Matthew Kelly said in his book, *The Rhythm of Life*: 'On the one hand, we all want to be happy. On the other hand, we all know the things that make us happy. But we don't do those things. Why? Simple. We are too busy. Too busy doing what? Too busy trying to be happy.'

So, I grabbed my planner, sat down on my couch, and committed to finding time – *making* time – for my daily personal development. I considered the options:

Maybe the evening?

My first thought was that maybe I could make time in the evenings, after work, or maybe late at night, after my fiancée goes to bed. But then I realized that the evening was really the only time I had to spend with her during the day. Not to mention that late at night is rarely when I'm at my best. I'm usually so tired that focusing is even more of a challenge than it usually is. In fact, I'm hardly coherent, let alone in an 'optimum' state of mind for personal development. Evening was not going to be the optimum time.

Possibly the afternoon?

Maybe I could schedule it in the middle of the day? Possibly on my lunch break, or somewhere in between, I could just find some 'extra' time. Well, that extra time just doesn't show up and the day usually gets away from us.

Aw, come on – not in the morning!

Then, I considered doing it in the morning – but I resisted. To say that I was *not* a morning person was a gross understatement. The fact was, I dreaded getting up in the morning, particularly waking up early, almost as much as I hated running. But the more I thought about it, the more a few things started to make sense.

First, by committing to my personal development in the morning, it would give me a positive motivational kick-start to my day. I could learn something new in the morning. I'd likely be more energized, more focused, and more motivated for the rest of my day. I remembered a blog post that I read on StevePavlina.com, titled 'The Rudder of the Day'. Steve, also the author of *Personal Development for Smart People*, stated: 'It's been said that the first hour is the rudder of the day. If I'm lazy or haphazard in my actions during the first hour after I wake up, I tend to have a fairly lazy and unfocused day. But if I strive to make that first hour optimally productive, the rest of the day tends to follow suit.'

Not to mention, by doing personal development in the morning, I wouldn't have all of the excuses that accumulate during the day (*I'm tired, I don't have time*, etc.) If I did it in the morning, before the rest of my life and my work got in the way, I could guarantee that it happened every single day.

Finally, I just didn't really see any better time to do it. Executing my personal development first thing in the morning was looking to be the most advantageous option, but it was already hard enough to drag myself out of bed every day at 6.00 am – *because I had to* – so the idea of getting up at 5.00 am seemed almost impossible to me. Feeling frustrated and a bit defeated, I was about to close my planner and forget the whole idea, when I heard the voice of my mentor, Kevin Bracy, in my head. Kevin always said, 'If you want your life to be different, you have to be willing to do something different first!'

Damn it. I knew Kevin was right, but that didn't make waking up early any easier. Committed to making a change, I decided to overcome my self-imposed, life-long limiting belief that I was not a morning person and wrote into my schedule that I would wake up at 5.00 am the next morning to do my first personal development routine.

Our second challenge: doing what's most impactful

Then I encountered another challenge – what was I going to do for that hour that was going to make the biggest impact and improve my life the fastest? I could read, but I'd done that before, and I wanted this to be special. I could exercise, but again, that wasn't getting my juices flowing. So, I pulled out a piece of blank paper and I wrote down all of the most life-changing personal development practices that I had learned over the years, but never implemented – at least never consistently. Activities like *meditation, affirmations, journaling, visualization*, as well as *reading* and *exercise*.

I chose the six activities that I thought would have the most immediate and dramatic impact on my life, assigned ten minutes each, and planned to try all six the next morning. The interesting thing was, looking at this list got me feeling motivated! All of a sudden the idea of waking up early went from something I dreaded to something more and more appealing. That night, I could hardly fall asleep, I was so excited for the morning to come!

When the alarm clock went off at 5.00 am, my eyes shot wide open and I sprung out of bed, feeling energized and excited! It was effortless, it was invigorating, and it reminded me of being a kid, waking up on Christmas morning. There had been no time in my life when waking up was easier, when I felt more energized and excited about my day, than I did as a kid on Christmas … until today.

The morning that transformed my entire life

Teeth brushed, face washed, and a glass of water in hand, I sat up straight on my living room couch at 5.05 am, feeling genuinely excited about my life for the first time in a long time. It was still dark outside, and something about that felt very empowering. I pulled out my list of life-changing personal development activities I had learned over the years but never implemented. One by one, I implemented each one.

Silence Sitting in silence, praying, meditating, and focusing on my breath, for ten minutes. I felt my stress melt away, felt a sense of calm come over my body and ease my mind. This was different from the typical chaos of my hectic mornings. For the first time in a long time, I felt *peaceful*.

Reading Having always made excuses why I couldn't find time to read, I was excited to make time this morning and start what I had always hoped could become a lifelong habit.

I grabbed Napoleon Hill's classic, *Think and Grow Rich*, off the shelf. Like most of my books, it was one that I had started, but never finished. I read for ten minutes, and picked up a few ideas that I was excited to implement that day. I was reminded that it only takes one idea to change your life, and I felt *motivated*.

Affirmations Having never before harnessed the power of affirmations, it felt amazing to finally read the 'self-confidence affirmation' from *Think and Grow Rich* aloud. The affirmation was a powerful reminder of the unlimited potential that was within me – and within each of us. I decided to write my own affirmation. I jotted down what I wanted, who I was committed to being, and what I was committed to doing to change my life. I felt *empowered*.

Visualization I grabbed the vision board off my wall (see Chapter 10 for more on vision boards). I had created it after watching the movie *The Secret*. I rarely took time to look at, let alone use it as the visualization tool it was intended to be. For ten minutes, my focus shifted from image to image, pausing at each one to close my eyes and feel, with every fibre of my being, what it would be like to manifest each into my life. I felt *inspired*.

Journaling Next, I opened one of the many blank journals I had purchased over the years. Like all of the others, I had failed to write in for more than a few days – a week at the most. On this day, I wrote what I was grateful for in my life. Almost immediately, I felt my depression lifting, like a heavy fog which had been weighing me down. It wasn't gone, but it felt lighter. The simple act of writing down the things I was grateful for lifted my spirits. I felt *grateful*.

Exercise Finally, I got up off the couch, remembering what I'd heard Tony Robbins say so many times: *motion creates emotion*. I dropped down and did push-ups until I couldn't do one more. Then I flipped over onto my back and did as many sit-ups as my out-of-shape abs would allow. With six minutes left on the clock, I inserted one of my fiancée's yoga videos into the DVD player, and enjoyed completing the first six minutes of it. I felt *energized*.

It was incredible! I had already experienced what was one of the most peaceful, motivating, empowering, inspiring, grateful, and energizing days of my life – and it was only 6.00 am!

Nothing short of a miracle

For the next few weeks, I continued to wake up at 5.00 am and follow through with my 60-minute personal development routine. Then, so incredibly happy with the way I was feeling and the progress I was making as a result of my morning routine, I wanted *more* of it! So, one night while getting ready for bed, I did what was unthinkable at the time; I set my alarm clock for 4:00 a.m. Falling asleep that night, I wondered if I was out of my mind.

Surprisingly, it was just as easy to wake up at 4:00 a.m. as it was 5:00 a.m., and waking up at either time was ten times easier than waking up on any day in my past, when I resisted waking up.

My stress levels dropped dramatically. I had more energy, clarity, and focus. I felt genuinely happy, motivated, and inspired. Thoughts of depression were a distant memory. You could say I was *back to my old self* again – although I was experiencing so much growth, so rapidly, that I was quickly surpassing any version of myself that I had ever been in the past. And with my newfound levels of energy, motivation, clarity, and focus I was able to easily set goals, create strategies and execute a plan to save my business and increase my income. Less than two months after my first 'Miracle Morning', my income was not only back to the level it had been at before the economy crashed, it was higher than ever before.

I knew this powerful morning personal development routine was something I would eventually start sharing with my private coaching clients, so I needed a name for it. Considering that the transformation I was experiencing was so profound and happening so fast – having gone from broke and depressed to financially secure and excited about life, in less than two months – that it felt like a miracle, the only appropriate name was *The Miracle Morning*.

Hey, if Katie can do it ...

A few weeks later, I was on a coaching call with Katie when she asked, 'Hal, how do you start your mornings?' Although I beamed as I told her about *The Miracle Morning* and the benefits of waking up an hour earlier than normal, she resisted. 'I don't know if I want to wake up any earlier, Hal. Trust me, I am *not* a morning person!'

However, Katie is always a good sport. She committed to waking up at 6.00 am – one hour earlier than normal – and giving *The Miracle Morning* a try. I offered her some encouragement and wished her luck.

On her coaching call one week later, Katie was on fire! When I asked if she actually woke up at 6.00 am every day to do *The Miracle Morning*, I got an unexpected reply. 'Nope. I woke up at 6. 00 am the first day, but you were right – I had such an awesome morning that I wanted to do it even earlier. So, I woke up at 5.00 am the rest of the week! Hal, it is amazing!'

Wow. I had to tell my other coaching clients about this.

Within a few short weeks, dozens of my clients were sharing with me that they were experiencing the same types of life-changing benefits during their own 'Miracle Mornings'. Some of my clients told their friends and co-workers about how *The Miracle Morning* was changing their life. It spread through the online world like wildfire. People start posting about *The Miracle Morning* on Facebook, tweeting about it on Twitter, and even proudly posting videos of themselves on YouTube, up early and doing *The Miracle Morning*.

Crazy, right?

Who the hell is Joe?

I started to realize there was something to this whole 'Miracle Morning' thing. I was on YouTube one day looking for one of my videos, and I put my name in the search. (Hey, don't judge – you know you've Googled yourself before.)

A video popped up that was titled 'Miracle Morning at Joe's'. It's of some guy that I've never seen before in my life. My first reaction was not very positive: 'Who the hell is Joe and who does he think he is copying my Miracle Morning?' I got a little defensive – not one of my finer moments. I just didn't know what to think. Boy, was I about to be pleasantly surprised, and humbled.

I hit play on the video and this is what I saw: 'Hello, it's your friend, Joe Diosana. Let's look at the time …' (Joe shows his alarm clock, which reads 5.41 am.) 'It is 5:41 in the morning, on Sunday, and you must be wondering, "Dude, Joe, what in the world are you doing up at 5.41 in the morning on a Sunday?" Well, check out miraclemorning.com. That's miraclemorning.com. Look at the information and download it. It feels like Christmas to me, honestly, and I've got a lot of energy. It's like Christmas every day now. Check it out, and I hope your life will be blessed.' (You can actually now watch Joe's infamous 43-second video, and many others, at www.MiracleMorning.com/SuccessStories/)

As I sat staring at my computer screen, mouth hanging wide open, I was in awe, almost in tears. It became clear to me that, while I never intended for *The Miracle Morning* to be anything more than my own morning routine, I now had a responsibility to share it with as many people as possible, so it could impact their lives the way it had mine. Although, at that point, I still had no idea just how *big* it would become.

A movement? Or is it an awakening?

It's been nearly five years since I told Katie about *The Miracle Morning* and watched Joe's video on YouTube. I've since received thousands of messages from people, all over the world, expressing their gratitude and enthusiasm for what *The Miracle Morning* has done for their lives. It truly has become a worldwide movement – a global *awakening* – made up of all types of individuals, each dedicated to waking up every day and giving themselves the gift of personal development. I now see the bigger picture, how *The Miracle Morning* can impact the world by enabling each of us become who we need to be to create the lives that we want; to positively influence the lives of others, and change the world around us.

Whether you call it a movement, an awakening, or what many are now referring to as *The Miracle Morning Mission*, it's about empowering people to transform their lives, their families, their communities, and the world by waking up every day and transforming themselves. Nearly every single day, hundreds more people are joining the mission and paying it forward by sharing it with others. I am still amazed at how many lives are being so deeply affected.

Some are even following Joe's lead and recording videos of themselves up early, doing *The Miracle Morning* (which usually includes a proud shot of their alarm clock – proving that they are indeed up early).

I am honoured and extremely grateful to have the opportunity to share this with so many people, in so many different capacities. In fact, *The Miracle Morning* is now one of my signature keynote messages and workshops, helping corporations, non-profits, salespeople, teachers, and high school and college students to increase their productivity, motivation and performance. Whether delivered as a keynote or workshop, it is a fresh approach to helping individuals and organizations improve their results while improving their attitude in the workplace. As you might guess, *The Miracle Morning* workshop is appropriately done in the morning, sometimes before the conference even begins.

Last, but not least

This book is an invitation to start taking your *self* to the next level so you can take your *success* to the next level (because it only happens in that order). By starting now, and making consistent, daily progress towards becoming the Level 10 person you need to be to create the Level 10 life you truly want and deserve, your success is inevitable.

3
The 95% reality check

One of the saddest things in life is to get to the end and look
back in regret, knowing that you could have been, done, and had
so much more.

Robin Sharma

The story of the human race is the story of men and women
selling themselves short.

Abraham Maslow

Every day you and I wake up, we face the same universal challenge: to overcome mediocrity and live to our full potential. It's the greatest challenge in human history – to rise above our excuses, do what's right, give our best and create the Level 10 life we truly want – the one with no limits, the one so few people ever get to live.

Unfortunately, most people never even come close. Approximately 95% of our society settles for far less than they want in life, wishing they had more, living with regret and never understanding that they could be, do, and have all that they want.

According to the Social Security Administration, if you take any 100 people at the start of their working careers and follow them for the next 40 years until they reach retirement age, here's what you'll find: only one will be wealthy; four will be financially secure; five will continue working, not because they want to but because they have to; 36 will be dead; and 54 will be broke and dependent on friends, family, relatives, and the government to take care of them.

Monetarily speaking, that's only 5% of us who will be successful in creating a life of freedom, and 95% who will continue to struggle their entire lives.

So the crucial question – the one that we must explore and find the answer to – is this: *what can we do now to ensure that we don't end up struggling, like the 95% majority will?*

Rising above mediocrity and joining the top 5%

The fact that you're reading this book tells me that you're ready for the next level in your life – that you're not okay with settling for less than you can have, be, and do anymore, just because nearly everyone else does.

Here are three simple, yet decisive steps to rise above mediocrity and join the top 5%:

Step 1: Acknowledge the 95% reality check

First, we must understand and acknowledge the reality that 95% of our society will never create and live the life they really want. We must embrace the fact that if we don't commit to thinking and living differently than *most people* now, we are setting ourselves up to endure a life of mediocrity, struggle, failure and regret – just like most people. Realize that this *will* include our own friends, family, and peers *if* we don't do something about it now and set an example of what's possible when we commit to fulfilling our potential.

Being average means to *settle* for less than you truly want and are capable of, and to *struggle* for your entire life. Every day, most people settle, and most people struggle on almost every level. Physically, mentally, emotionally, relationally, financially – you name it – most people wake up each day and struggle to create the levels of success, happiness, love fulfilment, health and financial prosperity that they truly desire.

Consider the following:

- **Physical**: Obesity is an epidemic. Potentially fatal diseases like cancer and heart disease are on the rise. The average person is exhausted, their physical energy levels at an all-time low. Most can't seem to generate enough energy to make it through a single day without consuming a few cups of coffee or an energy drink (the success of such products is further evidence of the degree to which people are struggling physically).
- **Mental and emotional**: More prescription drugs are being consumed every day in an attempt to combat disorders like depression, anxiety, and countless other

mental or emotional illnesses. Rarely do you turn on the TV without seeing an ad for some prescription drug. There's usually some good looking middle-aged couple, flying a kite on the beach with their dog. Then a man with a deep voice starts speaking gently, rattling off symptoms, followed by a list of potential side effects: 'Do you ever feel tired, sad, lonely, depressed, overweight, or anything else that you'd be willing to pay money to not feel anymore? Great, you're in luck – XYZ drug can help! Warning: may cause side effects such as bloating, constipation, diathermia, dizziness, dry mouth, dandruff, insomnia, narcolepsy, and many other things far worse than what it's actually supposed to help you with. So, don't wait – call the number on your screen today!'

- **Relationships**: It's well known that there is an epidemic of divorce in America, with one in two marriages failing. In other words, over half of those deeply in love couples, who stand before their friends and family and commit their lives to each other – *through the good times and the bad*, might I remind you – struggle to make it work. After more than 30 years of marriage, two of my favourite people – my mom and dad – recently divorced. I'm very present to the pain of this all too common relational struggle.
- **Financial**: Americans have more personal debt than at any other time in history. Most people aren't earning nearly as much money as they'd like to be earning. They're spending too much, not saving enough, and struggling financially.

It's no secret that most people are living life far below their potential. Once we can acknowledge that, it's crucial that we explore what causes most people to struggle and settle for mediocrity in their lives.

Step 2: Identify the causes of mediocrity

Once we've acknowledged that 95% of our society is settling for far less than they are capable of, struggling in almost every area, and not experiencing the levels of success, happiness, and freedom that they really want, the next crucial step is to understand *why*. To prevent it from happening to you, you must know what causes the average person to end up living a life of mediocrity.

If you were to ask the average person in this country – 40–50 years old, settling for less than they want, and struggling to be happy, pay their bills, etc. – if you were to ask them if *this* was their plan, their vision for their life, what do you think they would say? Do you think they envisioned their life being a struggle? Of course not! And that, my friend, is the *scary* part.

If 95% of our society is not living the life that they want, we *must* figure out what they did wrong or what they didn't do right, so that we don't end up living a life of mediocrity.

We don't want our lives to be a struggle. I want a life of freedom, where I get to wake up and do what I want, when I want, with whomever I want. I want to get out of bed every day and truly *love* my life. I want to *love* my work, and I want to *love* the people I get to share my life and work with. That's my definition of success. That kind of life doesn't just happen. It must be designed. If you want to live an extraordinary life as defined and designed by you, then you must identify the fundamental *causes of mediocrity* so you can prevent them from robbing you of the life you want.

The following are what I believe to be the most relevant causes of mediocrity and unfulfilled potential – the ones that have made and will continue to make the biggest impact on your life – and what you can do to defeat them:

THE CAUSES OF MEDIOCRITY (AND YOUR SOLUTIONS)

Rear-view mirror syndrome

One of the most crippling causes of mediocrity in life is a condition I call *rear-view mirror syndrome* (RMS). Our subconscious minds are equipped with a self-limiting rear-view mirror, through which we continuously relive and recreate our past. We mistakenly believe that who we *were* is who we *are*, thus limiting our true potential in the present, based on the limitations of our past.

As a result, we filter every choice we make – from what time we will wake up in the morning to which goals we will set to what we allow ourselves to consider possible for our lives – through the limitations of our past experiences. We want to create a better life, but sometimes we don't know how to see it any other way than how it's always been.

Research shows that on any given day, the average person thinks somewhere between 50,000 and 60,000 thoughts. The problem is that 95 percent of our thoughts are the same as the ones we thought the day before, and the day before that, and the day before that. It's no wonder most people go through life, day after day, month after month, year after year, and never change the quality of their lives.

Like old, worn baggage, we carry stress, fear, and worry from yesterday with us into today. When presented with opportunities, we quickly check our rear-view mirror to assess our past capabilities. 'No, I've never done anything like that before. I've never achieved at that level. In fact, I've failed, time and time again.'

When presented with adversity, we go back to our trusty rear-view mirror for guidance on how to respond. 'Yep, just my luck. This stuff always happens to me. I'm just going to give up; that's what I've always done when things get too difficult.'

If you are to move beyond your past and transcend your limitations, you must stop living out of your rear-view mirror and start imagining a life of limitless possibilities. Accept the paradigm: *my past does not equal my future.* Talk to yourself in a way that inspires confidence that not only is anything possible, but that *you* are capable and committed to making it so. It's not even necessary to believe it at first. In fact, you probably won't believe it. You might find it uncomfortable and that you resist doing it. That's okay. Repeat it to yourself anyway, and your subconscious mind will begin to absorb the positive self-affirmations (more on how to do this in Chapter 6).

Don't place unnecessary limitations on what you want for your life. Think bigger than you've allowed yourself to think up until this point. Get clear on what you truly want, condition yourself to the belief that it's possible by focusing on and affirming it every day, and then consistently move in the direction of your vision until it becomes your reality. There is nothing to fear, because you cannot fail – only learn, grow, and become better than you've ever been before.

Always remember that where you are is a result of who you *were*, but where you go depends entirely on who you choose to be, from this moment on.

Lack of purpose

If you ask the average person what their *life purpose* is, you will get a funny look or a response like, 'Gee, I dunno.' What if I asked you? What would you say? The average person can't articulate their life purpose – the compelling 'why' that drives them to wake up every day and do whatever it takes to fulfill their mission in life.

Rather, the average person takes life one day at a time, and has no higher purpose beyond merely surviving. Most people just focus on getting through the day, taking the path of least resistance, and pursuing short-term, short-lived pleasures along the way, while avoiding any pain or discomfort that might cause them to grow.

During the course of my seven-year career in direct sales, despite having broken numerous company sales records, I spent the first six of those seven years fighting the uphill battle of mediocrity, and losing more often than not. My results were inconsistent, and I consistently accepted far less than my best, until I finally figured out the secret to overcoming mediocrity: *live a life of purpose.*

After being inducted into my company's hall of fame, I was ready to move on and pursue my dream of becoming an author, speaker, and coach. However, *I had never achieved my full potential within the company.* I was about to leave the company with the mediocrity monkey on my back. It was sure to follow me into my next venture unless I did something about it.

Up until then, I didn't have a compelling life purpose that got me up in the morning even when I didn't *feel* like getting up. I had no purpose that drove me to get on the phone and call prospects, even when I didn't *need* more money. I decided in that moment that my life purpose for the next 12 months would be: *to become the person I need to be to create the success, freedom, and quality of life that I truly want.* I combined this with my other life purpose (yes, you can have more than one), which was to *selflessly add value to the lives of others* by assembling a team of 16 other sales reps. I led weekly conference coaching calls to support them in reaching their goals, free of charge, for the next 46 consecutive weeks.

Living every day in alignment with my two life purposes – constantly, consciously aligning my thoughts, words and actions with each purpose – not only did I have my best sales year ever (a 94% increase over my previous best), but I also led more reps to surpassing the highest performance level than at any other time in the company's 50-year history.

To defeat this cause of mediocrity, you need a *life purpose*, which can be any purpose you want. It can be anything that resonates with and inspires you to wake up every day and live in alignment with your purpose. Now, I totally understand that asking you to come up with your life's purpose right now may sound a bit overwhelming. Just remember that you get to make it up, and this first one can be something simple, even small. (e.g. 'I'm going to smile more so that I can bring a little more happiness to my life and to those around me.' Or, 'I'm going to ask every person I meet what I can do to help them, so that I can add value to more people's lives.') It will be your first step towards a bigger life purpose.

Keep in mind that you can change your life purpose at any time. As you grow and evolve, so will your purpose. What's important is that you choose a purpose – any purpose – and start living by it, now. You can even borrow one of the purposes I just shared with you (many of my coaching clients have).

Keep in mind that you're not supposed to 'figure out' what your purpose is, you get to make it up, create it, decide what you want it to be. In his bestselling book *The Rhythm of Life*, Matthew Kelly enlightens us to a universal life purpose that I believe we should all live by: *to become the best version of ourselves*. In other words, focus on growing and being the best you can be, pursuing your dreams and inspiring others to do the same. That's your purpose.

Schedule some time this week to think about and articulate your life purpose. Write it down where you'll see it every day. In fact, you'll have time to do this during your 'Miracle Morning'.

Always remember that when you are committed to a life purpose that is bigger than your problems, your problems become relatively insignificant and you will overcome them with ease.

Isolating incidents

One of the most prevalent, yet not-so-obvious causes of medi-ocrity is *isolating incidents*. We do this when we mistakenly assume that each choice we make, and each individual action we take, is only affecting that particular moment, or circum-stance. For example, you may think it's *no big deal* to miss a workout, procrastinate on a project, or eat fast food because you'll get a 'do-over' tomorrow. You make the mistake of think-ing that skipping that workout only affects that incident, and you'll make a better choice next time.

Nothing could be farther from the truth.

We must realize that the real impact and consequence of each of our choices and actions – and even our thoughts – is monumental, because every single thought, choice, and action is determining *who we are becoming*, which will ultimately determine the quality of our lives. As T. Harv Eker said in his best-selling book *Secrets of the Millionaire Mind*: 'How you do anything is how you do everything.'

Every time you choose to do the *easy* thing, instead of the *right* thing, you are shaping your identity, becoming the type of person who does what's easy, rather than what's right.

On the other hand, when you do choose to do the *right* thing and follow through with your commitments – especially when you don't *feel* like it – you are developing the extraor-dinary discipline (which most people never develop) neces-sary for creating extraordinary results in your life. As my good friend, Peter Voogd, often teaches his clients: 'Discipline creates lifestyle.'

For example, when the alarm clock goes off, and we hit the snooze button (the *easy* thing), most people mistakenly assume that this action is only affecting that moment. The reality is that this type of action is programming our subconscious mind with the instructions that it is okay for us to *not* follow through with the things we intended to do (more on that in the next chapter).

We must stop isolating incidents and start seeing the bigger picture. Realize that everything that we do affects who we're becoming, which is determining the life that we will ultimately create and live. When you see the big picture you start to take the alarm clock more seriously. When the buzzer goes off in the morning and you're tempted to snooze, you start thinking: *Wait – this is not who I want to become – someone who doesn't even have enough discipline to get out of bed in the morning. I'm getting up now, because I am committed to [waking up early, hitting my goals, creating the life of my dreams, etc.].*

Always remember that who you're becoming is far more important than what you're doing, and yet it is what you're doing that is determining who you're becoming.

Lack of accountability

The link between success and accountability is irrefutable. Virtually *all* highly successful people – from CEOs to professional athletes to the President of the United States – embrace a high degree of accountability. It gives them the leverage they need to take action and create results, even when they don't feel like it. Without it, we'd have a lot more pro-athletes skipping practice, and CEOs spending their days playing Words With Friends on their iPhones. I'm sure some are already doing that (I'm guilty of it occasionally), but we'd have a lot more.

Accountability is the act of being responsible to someone else for some action or result. Very little happens in this world, or in your life, without some form of accountability. Virtually every positive result you and I produced from birth to age 18 was thanks to the accountability provided for us by the adults in our lives (parents, teachers, bosses, etc.) Vegetables got eaten, homework was completed, teeth were brushed, we bathed and got to bed at a reasonable hour. If it weren't for the account-ability provided for us by our parents and teachers, we would have been uneducated, malnourished, sleep-deprived, dirty little kids! Nice way to reframe it, right?

Accountability has brought order to our lives and allowed us to progress, improve and achieve results we wouldn't have otherwise. Here's the problem: accountability was never something you and I asked for, but rather something that we endured as children, teens, and young adults. As it was forced upon us by adults, most of us unconsciously grew to resist and resent accountability altogether. Then, when we turned 18, we embraced every ounce of freedom we could get our hands on, continuing to avoid accountability like it was the plague, perpetuating a downward spiral into mediocrity, developing detrimental mindsets and habits such as laziness, deflecting responsibility, and taking short cuts – hardly a recipe for success.

Now that *we* are all grown up and striving to achieve worthy levels of success and fulfilment, we must take responsibility for initiating our own systems for accountability (or move back in with our parents). Your accountability system could be a professional coach, mentor, even a good friend or family member. The reality is that, statistically, 95% of the people that read any book don't implement what they learn, because no one is holding them accountable to do so. There is a way to change that.

[HIGHLY RECOMMENDED] GET AN ACCOUNTABILITY PARTNER

Have you ever had a day where you intended to exercise or go to the gym, but didn't go because you didn't *feel* like it? Sure, we all have. What about when you know someone is counting on you to meet them at the gym, or on the running trail – aren't you much more likely to follow through when you have someone else holding you accountable?

I strongly recommend teaming up with an 'accountability partner' while you read this book. This can be a friend, co-worker or family member that you simply share *The Miracle Morning* with by sending them to www.MiracleMorning.com so they can get a Miracle Morning 'Crash Course' (two free chapters of this book, as well as *The Miracle Morning* video and audio programmes – all for *free*.) That way, you have someone who is also committed to taking his or her life to the next level, and the two of you can support, encourage, and hold each other accountable.

You can even post an invitation on your Facebook wall, or to the highly supportive members of *The Miracle Morning* Community at www.MiracleMorning.com/resources. You might post something like: 'I'm looking for someone who wants to improve their life to be my accountability partner for *The Miracle Morning 30-day Life Transformation Challenge*. Check out www.MiracleMorning.com and let me know if you're interested.' Keep in mind that anyone who responds to this is the type of person you want to have in your circle of influence!

I'd urge you to make a commitment now to call, text or email a friend today, inviting them to join you on your 'Miracle Morning' journey, read the book with you, and be your accountability partner for *The Miracle Morning 30-Day Life Transformation Challenge* (see Chapter 10, or visit *The Miracle Morning* Community at www.MiracleMorning.com/resources to connect with fellow Miracle Makers and find your ideal accountability partner.

Mediocre circle of influence

Research has shown that we become like the average of the five people we spend the most time with. Who you spend your time with may be the single most determining factor in the person you become and in your quality of life. If you are surrounded with lazy, weak-minded, excuse-making people, you'll inevitably become like them. Spend time with positive, successful achievers and inevitably their attitudes and successful habits will reflect on you. You'll become more and more like them.

This is true in every area – success, health, happiness, weight, income. If all of your friends are generally happy and optimistic people, then you are going to naturally become more happy and optimistic just by being around them. If all of your friends are successful and earn over $100,000 a year – even if you enter their circle earning far less – you will automatically be pulled up by their level of thinking and influenced by the habits they've established to be successful.

On the contrary, if most of the people you associate with are constantly complaining and focused on the negative side of life, the odds are you will be too. If your friends are not striving to improve their lives, or if they're struggling financially, then they're not going to challenge or inspire you to do any better.

Unfortunately, there will be a lot of people who are trying to get ahead in life but keep getting pulled down by the people around them. This can be especially difficult when those people are your family. You must be strong and make sure you spend less time with people who don't encourage and challenge you to become the best you can be.

Seek out people who believe in you, admire you, and can help you get where you want to go in life. You must *actively* seek out such people to improve your circle of influence – they rarely just show up by chance. Here are some ways that you can do that:

- You can join an online community such as Meetup.com, where you can connect with like-minded people in your area who have similar interests. You can join an existing Meetup group, or start your own.
- If you are a business owner or a professional who markets any products or services, you can join a *business networking and referral marketing* group, the largest of which is BNI (www.bni.com). I was a

member of BNI for many years. It helped me grow my business and I always recommend it to others.

- If you are a student – high school, junior, high, or elementary school student – I highly recommend that you look into joining Boys & Girls Clubs of America by finding one of their 4,000 local Clubs at www.bgca.org. It is one of the best organizations for young people to set themselves on the road to success. Their mission is: To enable all young people, especially those who need us most, to reach their full potential as productive, caring, responsible citizens, and former Club members include Denzel Washington, Adam Sandler, Jennifer Lopez, and Shaquille O'Neal. Those aren't bad footsteps to follow if you want to be successful.

- As I've mentioned, we have an exceptionally positive, supportive, and highly interactive community you can join at www.MiracleMorning.com/resources. There you can connect and network with all types of like-minded individuals, all of whom are striving to take themselves, and their lives, to the next level while supporting others to do the same.

It is often said that 'misery loves company', but so does mediocrity. *Don't let the fears, insecurities, and limiting beliefs of others limit what's possible for you.* One of the most important commitments you will ever make is to proactively and continuously improve your circle of influence. Always seek people who will add value to your life and bring out the best in you. And of course, be that person for others.

This is another reason that it's so valuable for you to commit to inviting a friend, co-worker or family member to be your accountability partner and do *The Miracle Morning* with you. You'll be adding value to that person's life by helping them increase their level of personal development, which in turn will make them a better influence on you.

Lack of personal development

Jim Rohn has been one of my greatest mentors and has taught me many life-changing philosophies. In my opinion, none was greater than the idea that *our levels of success will rarely exceed our level of personal development, because success is something we attract by who we become.* In other words, your level of success – in every area of your life – will rarely exceed, and will usually *parallel,* your level of personal development (i.e. your knowledge, skills, beliefs, habits, etc.)

We touched on this earlier, but let's check in again. If you and I are measuring our levels of success in any area of our lives (health, finances, relationships, etc.) on a scale of one to ten – we both want Level 10 success, agreed? Okay, good.

Now, the problem is that most of us aren't investing time each day into developing ourselves into the Level 10 people that we need to be that are capable of attracting, creating, living, and sustaining the levels of success that we *say* we want. As a result, we struggle to attain the levels of health, happiness, energy, love, personal and professional success that we truly desire.

During *The Miracle Morning 30-Day Life Transformation Challenge* (see Chapter 10) you'll be given access to *The Miracle Morning 30-Day Life Transformation Challenge* 'Fast-Start Kit" where you'll be guided through the enlightening, sometimes painful, but surprisingly enjoyable process of assessing your levels of success in each area. Then, after you've gained a heightened level of clarity and self-awareness, you'll be able to clarify your Level 10 vision for each area of your life, and then establish your 'next level' goals for each area, so that you can immediately begin making significant progress towards your Level 10 vision.

The most extraordinary life you can imagine is available to you no matter what's happened in your past; just waiting for you to develop yourself into the person you need to be to be able to easily attract, create, and live that life.

The Miracle Morning will enable you to become that Level 10 person you need to be to easily and consistently, attract, create, and sustain Level 10 success that you want in every – yes, *every* – area of your life.

Always remember that when we fail to make time for personal development, we are forced to make time for pain and struggle. *The Miracle Morning* will give you that time for extraordinary personal development.

Lack of urgency

Arguably the single most significant cause of mediocrity and unfulfilled potential, which prevents 95% of our society from creating and living the life they truly want, is that most people have no sense of urgency to improve themselves so they can improve their lives. Human nature is to live with a 'someday' mindset and think *life will work itself out*. How's that working out for everybody?

This someday mindset is perpetual, and it leads to a life of procrastination, unfulfilled potential and regret. You wake up one day and wonder what the heck happened; how did your life end up *like this*? How did *you* end up like this?

One of the saddest things in life is to live with regret, knowing that you could have, be, and do so much more.

Remember this truth: *now* matters more than any other time in your life, because it's what you are doing today that is determining who you're becoming, and who you're becoming will always determine the quality and direction of your life.

If you don't make the commitment today to start becoming the person you need to be to create the extraordinary life you really want, what makes you think tomorrow – or next week, or next month, or next year – are going to be any different? They won't. And that's why you must draw your line in the sand.

Step 3: Draw your line in the sand

You've acknowledged and embraced the reality that 95% of society is struggling — and that if we don't commit to thinking and living differently than most people, we *will* end up struggling, like most people. You've identified the causes of mediocrity you absolutely need to remain aware of and avoid. The third step is to *draw your line in the sand.* Make a decision as to what *you* are going to start doing differently from this day forward.

Not tomorrow, not next week, or next month. You've got to make a decision *today* that you're ready to make the necessary changes to guarantee that you will be able to create the life you really want. To take your personal and professional success to the level they've never been before, you have to be willing to commit at a level you've never been committed before. Are you ready to make that commitment?

Your entire life changes the day that you decide you will no longer accept mediocrity for yourself. When you realize that today is the most important day of your life. When you decide that now matters more than any other time because it is who you are becoming each day based on the decisions that you are making and the actions that you are taking that is determining who you are going to be for the rest of your life.

The possibility of mediocrity exists for everyone, because being mediocre simply means choosing — whether consciously or unconsciously — to be the same as you've always been. Mediocrity has nothing to do with how you compare to other people; it's simply a result of *not* making the commitment to continuously learn, grow, and improve yourself. Whereas being extraordinary — which leads to extraordinary levels of success — is a result of choosing to learn, grow, and be a little bit better each day than you've been in the past.

We've all experienced the pain of regret — a result of thinking and talking ourselves into being, doing, and having less than we are capable of. Mediocre days turn into weeks. Weeks turn into months. Months inevitably turn into years, and if we don't start improving who we are and what we do, now, then our self-created fate will be a life of mediocrity and unfulfilled potential.

The reality is that if we don't change *now*, our life won't change. If we don't get better, our life won't get better. And if we don't consistently invest time into our self-improvement, our life will not improve. Yet, most of us wake up every day and stay the same.

I think you want more for your life. I know I do. If you're being completely honest with yourself, you truly want to live an extraordinary life. That doesn't necessarily mean being rich or famous. Everyone's dream is different. What it does mean is living your definition of an extraordinary life. A life where you get to call the shots, and live life on your terms, with the freedom to do, be, and have everything you've ever wanted for your life. No excuses. No regrets. Just an incredible, meaningful, and exciting life!

As stated so truthfully by bestselling author, Robin Sharma: 'One of the saddest things in life is to get to the end and look back in regret, knowing that you could have been, done, and had so much more.' While this is the self-imposed fate of the masses, it absolutely does not have to be yours. Today you can draw your line in the sand. You can decide that mediocrity is no longer acceptable for *you*. You can claim your greatness. You can choose to become the person you need to be to create the extraordinary life that you truly want. Your life can be filled with an abundance of energy, love, health, happiness, success, financial prosperity, and everything else that you've ever imagined having, doing, or being. *The Miracle Morning* can give you that life.

But first, an important question...

4
Why did YOU wake up this morning?

You've got to get up every morning with determination if you're going to go to bed with satisfaction.

George Lorimer

Your first ritual that you do during the day is the highest leveraged ritual, by far, because it has the effect of setting your mind, and setting the context, for the rest of your day.

Eben Pagan

Why did you bother getting out of bed this morning? Think about that for a second ... Why do you wake up most mornings? Why do you leave the comfort of your warm, cozy bed? Is it because you *want* to? Or do you delay waking up until you absolutely *have* to?

If you're like most people, you wake up to the incessant beeping of an alarm clock each morning and reluctantly drag yourself out of bed because you *have* to be somewhere, do something, answer to – or take care of – someone else. Given the choice (do you have a choice?) most people would continue sleeping.

So naturally, we rebel. We hit the snooze button and resist the inevitable act of waking up, unaware that our resistance is sending a message to the universe that we'd rather lie there in our beds – unconscious – than consciously and actively live and create the lives we *say* that we want. Most of us have resigned ourselves to a certain level of mediocrity and unfulfilled potential. We don't like it. We don't feel good about it. We know that there is absolutely another level of success, achievement and fulfilment that's possible for us, but we feel stuck, and we don't know what to do to get ourselves unstuck.

You snooze, you lose: the truth about waking up

The old saying, 'You snooze, you lose' may have a much deeper meaning than any of us realized. When you delay waking up until you *have* to – meaning you wait until the last possible moment to get out of bed and start your day – consider that what you're actually doing is resisting your life. Every time you hit the snooze button, you're in a state of resistance to your day, to your life, and to waking up and creating the life you say you want. Think about the kind of negative energy that surrounds you when you begin your day with resistance, when you respond to the sound of the alarm clock with internal dialogue along the lines of, 'Oh no, it's time already. I *have* to wake up. I don't want to wake up.' It's as if you're saying, 'I don't want to live my life, at least not to the fullest.'

Many people who suffer from depression report that the morning time is the most difficult. They wake up with dread. Sometimes it is because of a job they feel obligated to go to, or due to a relationship that is failing. Some people feel this way simply due to the nature of depression and its ability to weigh on a person's mind, emotions, and heart without needing a specific reason. The tone of our morning has a powerful impact on the tone of the rest of our day. It becomes a cycle: waking up with despair, spending the day continuing to feel that way, going to sleep feeling anxious or depressed, then repeat the cycle of melancholy the next day.

Not only are people missing out on the abundance of clarity, energy, motivation, and personal power that comes from waking up each day *on purpose*, but their resistance to this inevitable daily act is a defiant statement to the universe that they would rather lie in bed, unconscious, than to create and live the life they desire.

On the other hand, when you wake up each day with passion and purpose, you join the small percentage of high achievers who are living their dreams. Most importantly, you will be happy. By simply changing your approach to waking up in the morning, you will literally change everything. But don't take my word for it – trust these famous early risers: Oprah Winfrey, Tony Robbins, Bill Gates, Howard Schultz, Deepak Chopra, Wayne Dyer, Thomas Jefferson, Benjamin Franklin, Albert Einstein, Aristotle, and far too many more to list here.

No one ever taught us that by learning how to consciously set our intention to wake up each morning with a genuine desire – even enthusiasm – to do so, we can change our entire lives.

If you're just snoozing every day until the last possible moment you have to head off to work, show up for school, or take care of your family, and then coming home and zoning out in front of the television until you go to bed (this used to be my daily routine), I've got to ask you: *When are you going to develop yourself into the person you need to be to create the levels of health, wealth, happiness, success and freedom that you truly want and deserve? When are you going to actually live your life instead of numbly going through the motions looking for every possible distraction to escape reality? What if your reality – your life – could finally be something that you can't wait to be conscious for?*

There is no better day than today for us to give up who we've been for who we can become, and upgrade the life we've been living for the one we really want. There is no better book than the one you are holding in your hands to show you how to become the person you need to be who is capable of quickly attracting, creating and sustaining the life you have always wanted.

How much sleep do we really need?

The first thing experts will tell you about how many hours of sleep we need is that there is no 'magic number'. The amount of sleep that is ideal varies for every individual, and is influenced by factors such as age, genetics, overall health, how much exercise a person gets, and many others. While you may be at your absolute best sleeping seven hours a night, someone else may clearly need nine hours to have a happy, productive life.

According to the National Sleep Foundation, some research has found that *long* sleep durations (nine hours or more) are also associated with increased morbidity (illness, accidents) and even mortality (death.) This research also found that variables such as depression were significantly associated with long sleep.

Since there is such a wide variety of opposing evidence from countless studies and experts, and since the amount of sleep needed varies from person to person, I'm not going to attempt to make a case that there is one *right* approach to sleep. Instead, I'll share my own real-world results, from personal experience and experimentation, and from studying the sleep habits of some of the greatest minds in history. I'll warn you, some of this may be somewhat controversial.

How to wake up with more energy (on less sleep)

Through experimenting with various sleep durations – as well as learning those of many other *The Miracle Morning* practitioners who have tested this theory – I've found that how our sleep affects our biology is largely affected by our own personal *belief* about how much sleep we need. In other words, how we feel when we wake up in the morning – and this is a very important distinction – is not solely based on how many hours of sleep we got, but significantly impacted by how we told ourselves we were going to feel when we woke up.

For example, if you *believe* that you need eight hours of sleep to feel rested, but you're getting into bed at midnight and have to wake up at 6.00 am, you're likely to tell yourself, 'Geez, I'm only going to get six hours of sleep tonight, but I need eight. I'm going to feel exhausted in the morning.' Then, what happens as soon as your alarm clock goes off and you open your eyes and you realize it's time to wake up? What's the first thought that you think? It's the same thought you had before bed! 'Geez, I only got six hours of sleep. I feel exhausted.' It's a self-fulfilling, self-sabotaging prophecy. If you tell yourself you're going to feel tired in the morning, then you are absolutely going to feel tired. If you believe that you need eight hours to feel rested, then you're not going to feel rested on anything less. But what if you changed your beliefs?

The mind–body connection is a powerful thing, and I believe we must take responsibility for every aspect of our lives, including the power to wake up every day feeling energized, regardless of how many hours of sleep we get.

I've experimented with various durations of sleep – from as little as four hours to as many as nine. The other variable in my experimentation was actively telling myself how I was going to feel in the morning, based on the amount of hours I slept. First, I tried each duration of sleep, telling myself before bed that I was *not* getting enough sleep, and that I was going to feel exhausted in the morning.

On four hours of sleep, I woke up feeling exhausted. On five hours of sleep, I woke up feeling exhausted. On six hours of sleep, you guessed it – exhausted.

Seven hours ... Eight hours ... Nine hours ... The hours of sleep I got didn't change how I felt when the alarm clock went off in the morning. As long as I told myself before bed that I wasn't getting enough sleep, and that I was going to feel tired in the morning, that's exactly how I felt.

Then, I again experimented with each duration – from nine hours to four hours – this time reciting a bedtime affirmation and telling myself that I was going to wake up feeling *energized* in the morning: 'Thank you for giving me these *five* hours of sleep tonight. *Five* hours is exactly what I need to feel rested and energized in the morning. My body is capable of miraculous things, the least of which is generating an abundance of energy from five restful hours of sleep. I believe that I create my experience of reality, and I choose to create waking up tomorrow feeling energized and excited to take on my day, and I'm grateful for that.'

What I found was that whether I got nine, eight, seven, six, five, or even just four hours of sleep, as long as I consciously decided, before bed, that I was getting the perfect amount of sleep – that the hours were going to energize my body to feel wonderful in the morning – I consistently woke feeling better than I ever had before. However, don't take my word for it. I encourage you to experiment with this yourself.

So, how many hours of sleep do you *really* need? You tell me. Now, if you really struggle with falling or staying asleep, and it is a concern for you, I highly recommend getting a copy of Shawn Stevenson's book, *Sleep Smarter: 21 Proven Tips to Sleep Your Way to a Better Body, Better Health, and Bigger Success*. It's one of the best, most well researched books that I've seen on the topic of sleep.

The secret to making every morning feel like Christmas

Think back to a time in your life when you were genuinely excited to wake up in the morning. Maybe it was to catch an early flight for a vacation that you had been anticipating for months. Maybe it was your first day at a new job, or your first day of school. Maybe it was your wedding day, or your last birthday. Personally, I can't think of any time in my life when I was more excited to wake up in the morning – regardless of how much sleep I got – than when I was a kid, every year on Christmas morning. Maybe you can relate?

Whatever the occasions have been that have had you excited to wake up in the morning, how did you feel when those mornings arrived? Did you have to drag yourself out of bed? Doubtful. On mornings like these, we can't wait to wake up! We do so feeling energized and genuinely excited. We quickly heave the covers off and spring to our feet, ready to take on the day! Imagine if this is what *every day* of your life was like. Shouldn't it be? It can.

The Miracle Morning is largely about recreating that experience of waking up feeling energized and excited, and doing it every single day of your life — for the rest of your life! It's about getting out of bed with purpose — not because you *have* to, but because you genuinely want to — and dedicating time each day to developing yourself into the person you need to be to create the most extraordinary, fulfilling, and abundant life you can imagine. *The Miracle Morning* is already doing just that for thousands of people around the world. People just like you.

5
The five-step snooze-proof wake-up strategy (for all of the snooze-aholics)

If you really think about it, hitting the snooze button in the morning doesn't even make sense. It's like saying '*I hate getting up in the morning, so I do it over, and over, and over again.*'

Demetri Martin

I'd like mornings better if they started later.

Unknown

First, let me just say that if it wasn't for this strategy that I'm about to share with you, I would still be sleeping – or snoozing – through my alarm clock every morning, and what's even more detrimental, I would still adhere to my old limiting belief, claiming that I was not a 'morning person'.

It's been said that nobody actually *likes* waking up early, but everyone loves the feeling of having woken up early. Kind of like exercising – many of us struggle to get ourselves to the gym, but all of us love the feeling of having gone to the gym. Waking up early, especially when done with *purpose*, always starts you off feeling empowered for your day.

Increasing your wake-up motivation level (WUML)

For most of us, when the alarm clock sounds each morning, we are woken from a dead sleep. Leaving the comfort of our beds is the least appealing thing to do. If you were to rate your level of motivation as it pertained to waking up – a.k.a. your wake-up motivation level (WUML) – at the moment the alarm clock starts incessantly beeping, on a scale of 1–10 (10 being ready to wake up and embrace the day, and 1 meaning you want nothing more than to go back to sleep), most of us would probably rate our WUML close to a 1 or a 2. It's perfectly natural, when you're still half asleep, to want to hit the snooze button and keep on sleeping.

The challenge is, how do you give yourself the motivation you need to wake up early and create an extraordinary day, when your wake-up motivation level is only at a one or two when your alarm clock sounds?

The answer is simple: *one step at a time*. Here are my five simple, snooze-proof steps to making waking up in the morning – even *early* in the morning – easier than ever before.

Step 1: Set your intentions before bed

The first key to waking up is to remember this: Your *first thought in the morning is usually the last thought you had before you went to bed*. For example, we've all had nights where we could hardly fall asleep because we are so excited about waking up the next morning. Whether it was Christmas Eve, the night before your birthday, your first day of school, starting a new job, or going on vacation – as soon as the alarm clock sounds, you open your eyes with enthusiasm and excitement to get out of bed and embrace the day!

On the other hand, if your last thought before bed was something like, 'I can't believe I have to get up in six hours; I'm going to be exhausted in the morning!' then your first thought when the alarm clock goes off is likely along the lines of, 'Oh my gosh, it's already been six hours? Nooo! I just want to keep sleeping!'

So, the key is to consciously decide every night to actively and mindfully create a positive expectation for the next morning. For help on this and to get the precise words to say before bed to create your powerful intentions, download *The Miracle Morning* 'Bedtime Affirmation' free at www.MiracleMorning.com/resources.

Step 2: Move your alarm clock across the room

If you haven't already, move your alarm clock as far away from your bed as possible. This forces you to rise from bed and engage your body in movement. Motion creates energy, so when you get up and out of bed it naturally helps you wake up.

If you keep your alarm clock next to your bed, then you are still in a partial sleep-state when the alarm goes off, and it makes it much more difficult to wake yourself up. I'm sure you can probably relate to rolling over – still half-asleep – and turning the alarm clock off without even realizing that it went off. I know that on many occasions I've even convinced myself that my alarm clock was merely part of the dream I was having.

Simply forcing yourself to get out of bed to turn off the alarm clock will instantly take your wake-up motivation level from a WUML-1 to a WUML-2. However, you'll still likely be feeling more sleepy than not. So ...

Step 3: Brush your teeth

I know, I know. *Really Hal, you're telling me to brush my teeth?* Yes. The point is that you're doing mindless activities for the first few minutes and simply giving your body time to wake up. So, after turning off your alarm clock, go directly to the bathroom sink to brush your teeth and splash some warm (or cold) water on your face. This simple activity will increase your wakeup motivation level from a WUML-2 to a WUML-3 or WUML-4. Now that your mouth is minty fresh, it's time to...

Step 4: Drink a full glass of water

It's crucial that you hydrate yourself first thing every morning. After six to eight hours without water, you'll naturally be mildly dehydrated, and dehydration causes fatigue. Often when people feel tired – at any time of the day – what they really need is more water, not more sleep.

Start by getting a glass of water (or you can do what I do, and fill it up the night before so it's already there for you in the morning), and drink it as fast as is comfortable for you. The objective is to rehydrate your body and mind as fast as possible, to replace the water you were deprived of during the hours you slept.

When you drink a glass of water and hydrate yourself, your wake-up motivation level goes from a WUML-3 or WUML-4 to a WUML-4 or WUML-5.

Step 5: Get dressed in your workout clothes

Last but not least, get dressed in your exercise clothes, so you're ready to leave your bedroom and immediately engage in your Miracle Morning. Some people prefer to start their day by jumping into the shower, but I believe we should *earn* our morning shower by breaking a sweat first!

Morning exercise is crucial to maximizing your potential, because it puts you into a peak mental, physical, and emotional state so that you can win the day. We'll cover exercise in more depth in the next chapter.

It only takes about five minutes to execute these five simple steps, and when you do, your wake-up motivation level should naturally be at a WUML-5 or WUML-6. At that point it requires much less discipline to stay awake for your Miracle Morning. If you were to try and make that commitment at the time your alarm clock went off – while you were at a WUML1 – it would be a much more difficult decision to make.

Here's a quick review of the *five-step snooze-proof wake-up strategy* to make it signficantly easier to wake up and stay awake:

1 **Set your intentions the night before**: This is the *most important* step. Remember: your first thought in the morning is usually the last thought you had before bed, so take responsibility for creating genuine excitement for the next morning, every night before bed.

2 **Keep your alarm clock across the room**: Remember – movement creates energy!

3 **Brush your teeth**: Use a mouthwash for extra umph!

4 **Drink a Full Glass of Water**: Hydrate yourself, ASAP.

5 **Get in your workout clothes**: Earn your A.M. shower!

Miracle Morning bonus wake-up tips

Keep in mind that although this strategy has proven to be work for thousands of people, these five steps are not the *only* way to make waking up in the morning easier. Here are a few other tips I've heard from fellow Miracle Morning practitioners:

- **TMM bedtime affirmations:** If you haven't done this yet, you can take a minute now to go to www.MiracleMorning.com/resources and download the re-energizing, intention-setting 'Miracle Morning Bedtime Affirmations', for free.
- **Set a timer for your bedroom lights:** One of our *Miracle Morning* Community members sets his bedroom lights on a timer (you can buy an 'appliance timer' online or at your local hardware store). As his alarm goes off, the lights come on in the room. What a great idea. It's a lot easier to fall back asleep when it's dark, so having the lights come on tells your mind and body that it's time to wake up. Regardless of whether or not you use a timer, be sure to turn your light on first thing when your alarm goes off.

Set a timer for your bedroom heater: Another fan of *The Miracle Morning* said that in the winter, she kept a bedroom heater on an appliance timer set to go off 15 minutes before she woke up. She kept it cold at night, but warm for waking up so that she wouldn't be tempted to crawl back under her covers to avoid the cold. She said it made a huge difference!

Feel free to add to or customize your *snooze-proof wake-up strategy*, and if you have any tips you're open to sharing, I'd love to hear them. Please feel free to contact me directly in *The Miracle Morning* Community (on Facebook) at www.MiracleMorning.com/resources.

It's all about having an effective, pre-determined, step-by-step stratcgy to increase your *wake-up motivation level* in the morning. Don't wait to try this! Start *tonight* by reading *The Miracle Morning* 'Bedtime Affirmation', moving your alarm clock across the room, setting a glass of water on your nightstand, and committing to the other two steps for the morning.

6

The Life S.A.V.E.R.S: Six practices guaranteed to save you from a life of unfulfilled potential

Success is something you attract by the person you become.

Jim Rohn

An extraordinary life is all about daily, continuous improvements in the areas that matter most.

Robin Sharma

Stressed. Overwhelmed. Frustrated. Unfulfilled. Blah.

These are a few unpleasant words that provide a rather unfortunate, but fairly accurate description of how the average person feels about his or her life, far too often.

You and I are undoubtedly living in one of the most prosperous, advanced times in human history, with more opportunities and resources available to us than ever before. Yet most of us aren't tapping into the unlimited potential that is within every single one of us. I'm not okay with that. Are you?

The potential gap

Have you ever felt like the life you want to live and the person you know you can be are just beyond your grasp? Do you ever feel like you're chasing your potential – you know it's there, you can see it – but you can never quite catch it? When you see people who are excelling in an area that you're not, does it seem like they've got it all figured out – like they must know something that you don't know, because if you knew it, then you'd be excelling in that area too?

Most of us live our lives on the wrong side of a huge gap in our potential, a gap which separates who we are from who we can become. We are often frustrated with ourselves, our lack of consistent motivation, effort and results in one or more areas of life. We spend too much time *thinking* about the actions we should be taking to create the results that we want, but then we don't take those actions. We all know what we need to do; we just don't consistently do what we know. Can you relate?

This *potential gap* varies in size from person to person. You may feel like you're very near your current potential and that a few tweaks could make all the difference. Or you might feel the opposite – like your potential is so far away from who you've been that you don't even know where to start. Whatever the case is for you, know that it is absolutely possible and attainable for you to live your life on the right side of your potential gap and become the person you are capable of becoming.

Whether you are currently sitting on the wrong side of the grand canyon of your potential, wondering how you're going to get to the other side, or you've been working your way across the canyon but are stuck at a plateau and haven't been able to close that gap and get to the next level – this chapter will introduce you to six tools that will enable you to go from where you are – accepting less from yourself than what you know is possible – to developing yourself into the person you *know* you can become.

Your life is not what you think it is

Most of us are so busy trying to manage, maintain, or even just survive our life 'situation' that we don't make the time to focus on what's most important – our *life*. What's the difference? Our life situation is the set of *external* circumstances, events, people, and places that surround us. It's not who we are. We are more than our life situation.

Your *life* is who you are at the deepest level. Your life is made up of the *internal* components, attitudes, and mindsets that can give you the power to alter, enhance, or change your life situation at any given moment.

Your *life* is made up of the *physical, intellectual, emotional* and *spiritual* parts that make up every human being – or PIES for short.

The *physical* includes things like your body, health and energy. The *intellectual* incorporates your mind, intelligence and thoughts. The *emotional* takes into account your emotions, feelings, and attitudes. The *spiritual* includes intangibles such as your spirit, soul, and the unseen higher power that oversees all.

Your *life* is where your ability to create new feelings, per-spectives, beliefs, and attitudes in your 'inner' world lies, so that you can create or alter the circumstances, relationships, results, and anything else in the 'external' realm of your life situation. As many sages have taught us: *our outer world is a reflection of our inner world.* By focusing time and effort each day on developing your PIES, and constantly becoming a better version of yourself, your life situation will inevitably – almost automatically – improve.

I can assure you that through my own transformative journey – from the depths of mediocrity, justifying my excuses and living most areas of my life somewhere in between mediocre and average, to achieving goals that at one time seemed impossible for me – your commitment to daily personal development will be as instrumental for your transformation as it was for mine.

Time to save the life you deserve to live

For too many people, the extraordinary, fulfilling, abundant life that they really want – our Level 10 life – eludes them because they're so overwhelmed and overrun with their day-to-day life situation. Their life situation is eating up all of their time so that their life, and what matters most, isn't getting attended to.

In order to save your Level 10 life from being neglected and limited by the demands of your life situation – which ultimately leads to a life of regret, unfulfilled potential, and even mediocrity – you must prioritize and dedicate time each day to your personal development. Enter *The Miracle Morning Life S.A.V.E.R.S.* – a set of six simple, *life*-enhancing, *life*-changing daily practices, each of which develops one or more of the *physical*, *intellectual*, *emotional* and *spiritual* aspects of your life, so that you can become who you need to be to create the life you want.

Remember, when you change your inner world – your *life* – then your outer world – your *life situation* – will improve in parallel.

Here are six powerful, proven personal development practices known as the Life S.A.V.E.R.S. that you'll use to gain access to the powerful forces – already within you – that will enable you to alter, change, or transform any area of your life. Let's look at each of the six personal development tools that make up the Life S.A.V.E.R.S. and how each will help you become the person you need to be to easily attract, create, and live the most extraordinary life you have ever imagined.

The first 'S' of S.A.V.E.R.S.

Nope, it's not 'sleep'. Sorry. While I know many people would love it if they could sleep their way to success, unless you have been cryogenically frozen and are awaiting a large inheritance at the time of being thawed out – life just doesn't work that way.

S is for Silence

In the attitude of silence the soul finds the path in a clearer light, and what is elusive and deceptive resolves itself into crystal clearness.

Mahatma Gandhi

You can learn more in an hour of silence than you can in a year from books.

Matthew Kelly

Silence is the first practice of the Life S.A.V.E.R.S. and may be one of the most significant areas for improvement for our noisy, fast-paced and over-stimulated lifestyles. I'm referring to the life-transforming power of *purposeful silence*. 'Purposeful' simply means that you are engaging in a period of silence with a highly beneficial purpose in mind – not just for the heck of it. As Matthew Kelly so eloquently states in his bestselling book *The Rhythm of Life*: 'You can learn more in an hour of silence than you can in a year from books.' That's a powerful statement from a very wise man.

If you want to immediately reduce your stress levels, to begin each day with the kind of calm, clarity and peace of mind that will allow you to stay focused on what's most important in your life, and even dance on the edge of enlightenment – do the opposite of what *most people* do – start every morning with a period of purposeful silence.

The life-enhancing benefits of silence have been well documented throughout the ages. From the power of prayer, to the magic of meditation, some of the greatest minds in history have used purposeful silence to transcend their limitations and create extraordinary results.

How do your mornings usually begin?

Do you invest time in centring yourself and creating an optimum state of mind to lead you through the rest of the day? Or do you usually wait to wake up until you've got something to do? Do the words *calm*, *peaceful*, or *rejuvenating* describe your average morning? If they do, congratulations! You're already a step ahead of the rest of us.

For most of us, words like *rushed*, *hectic*, *stressful* or even *chaotic* might best describe our typical morning. For others, *slow*, *lazy* and *lethargic* might be a more accurate description of how our day begins. Which of these scenarios best describe your mornings?

Mornings, for most of us, are typically pretty hectic and rushed. We're usually running around trying to get ready for the day, and our minds are often plagued with internal chatter about *what we have to do, where we have to go, who we have to see, what we forgot to do, the fact that we're running late, a recent argument with our significant other or family member.*

For others, we have trouble just getting going on most mornings. We feel sluggish, lazy, and unproductive. So, for the great majority of us, the mornings are either stressful and rushed, or slow and unproductive. Neither of these represents the optimum way to start your day.

Silence is one of the best ways to immediately reduce stress, while increasing your self-awareness and gaining the clarity that will allow you to maintain your focus on your goals, priorities, and what's most important for your life, each and every day.

Here are some of my favourite activities to choose from and practise during my period of silence, in no particular order, followed by a simple meditation to get you started:

- Meditation
- Prayer
- Reflection
- Deep Breathing
- Gratitude

Some mornings I do just one of these activities, and other mornings I combine them. All of these practices will relax your mind and body, calm your spirit, and allow you to be totally present and open to receiving the benefits that will come from the remaining *Life S.A.V.E.R.S.* which make up the rest of your Miracle Morning.

It is very important that you don't stay in bed for this, and preferably that you leave your bedroom altogether. The problem with staying in bed – or even in your bedroom, where your comfy bed is within your line of sight – is that it's too easy to go from *sitting* in silence, to slouching, to falling back asleep. I always sit on my living room couch, where I already have everything set up that I need for my Miracle Morning. My affirmations, journal, yoga DVD, the book I'm currently reading – everything has its place and is ready for me each day so that, in the morning, it's easy to jump right in and engage in my Miracle Morning, without having to search for anything.

MEDITATION

Since there are plenty of great books, articles, and websites that concentrate on meditation, I won't go into too much detail in describing the proven benefits and the various approaches to meditating. Instead, I'll just mention a few of what I believe are the most significant benefits, and give you simple step-by-step meditation that you can begin immediately.

The essence of meditation is simply silencing or focusing the mind for a period of time. You may or may not be aware of all the extraordinary health benefits of meditating. Study after study shows that meditation can be more effective than *medication*. Studies link regular meditation to improvements in metabolism, blood pressure, brain activity, and other bodily functions. It can alleviate stress and pain, promote sleep, enhance focus and concentration, and even increase lifespan. Meditation also requires very little time. You can take advantage of the benefits of meditation in just a few minutes a day.

Well-known celebrities, CEOs and highly successful people like Jerry Seinfeld, Sting, Russell Simmons, Oprah and many more have publically stated that regular, often daily, meditation has become an invaluable part of their life. Tupperware CEO Rick Goings told the *Financial Times* that he tried to meditate for at least 20 minutes every day, stating, 'For me, it's a practice that not only burns off stress, but gives me fresh eyes to clarify what's really going on and what really matters'. Oprah told Dr. Oz that Transcendental Meditation has helped her 'connect with that which is God', according to the Huffington Post.

There are many genres and types of meditation, but generally speaking you can divide them into two categories: 'guided' and 'individual' meditations. Guided meditations are those in which you listen to another person's voice and receive instructions to help guide your thoughts, focus, and awareness. Individual meditations are simply those you do on your own, without assistance from anyone else.

Miracle Morning meditation

Here is a simple, step-by-step individual meditation that you can use during your Miracle Morning, even if you've never meditated before.

Before beginning your meditation, it's important to prepare your mindset and set your expectations. This is a time for you to quiet your mind and let go of the compulsive need to constantly be *thinking* about something – either reliving the past, stressing or worrying about the future – but never living fully in the present. This is the time to let go of your stresses, take a break from worrying about your problems, and be fully present in *this* moment. It is a time to access the essence of who you *truly* are – to go deeper than what you have, what you do, or the labels you've accepted as 'who you are' – which most people have never even attempted to do. Accessing this essence of *who you truly are* is often referred to as 'just being'. Not thinking, not doing, just *being*. If this sounds foreign to you, or too 'new age' that's okay. I used to feel the same way. It's probably just because you've never tried it before. But thankfully, you're about to.

Find a quiet, comfortable place to sit. You can sit up straight on the couch, on a chair, on the floor, or sit on a pillow for added comfort.

Sit upright, cross-legged. You can close your eyes, or you can look down at the ground, approximately two feet in front of you.

Begin by focusing on your breath, taking slow, deep breaths. In through the nose, out through the mouth, and be sure to breathe into your belly, rather than your chest. The most effective breathing should cause your belly to expand, and not your chest.

Now, start pacing your breath; in slowly on a count of three seconds (one, one-thousand, two, one-thousand, three, one-thousand) … hold it in for three seconds (one, one-thousand, two, one-thousand, three, one-thousand) … and then breathe out slowly on a count of three seconds (one, one-thousand, two, one-thousand, three, one- thousand). Feel your thoughts and emotions settling down as you focus on your breath. Be aware that as you attempt to quiet your mind, thoughts will still come in to pay a visit. Simply acknowledge them, then let them go, always returning your focus to your breath.

Remember, this is a time for you to let go of your compulsive need to *constantly* be thinking about something. This is a time to let go of your stress and take a break from worrying about your problems. This is the time to be fully present in *this* moment. This is often referred to as just *being*. Not thinking, not doing, just being. Continue to follow your breaths, and imagine inhaling positive, loving, peaceful energy, and exhaling all of your worries and stress. Enjoy the quiet. Enjoy the moment. Just breathe … *Just be*.

If you find that you have a constant influx of thoughts, it may be helpful for you to focus on a single word or a phrase, and repeat it over and over again to yourself, as you inhale and exhale. For example, you might try something like: (*On the inhale*) 'I breathe in peace ...' (*As you exhale*) 'I breathe out love ... I breathe in peace...' (*Inhale*)... 'I breathe out love...' (*Exhale*)... You can swap the words *peace* and *love* with whatever you feel like you need bring more of into your life (*confidence, faith, energy, belief*, etc.), and whatever you feel like you want to give more of to the world.

Meditation is a gift you can give to yourself every day. It truly is an incredible gift. My time spent meditating has become one of my favourite parts of my day. It is a time to be at peace, to experience gratitude, and a time of freedom from our day-to-day stressors and worries. Think of daily meditation as a temporary vacation from your problems. While your problems will still be there when you finish your daily meditation, you'll find that you are much more centred and better equipped to solve them.

Final thoughts on silence

There's no single right way to spend time in silence. You can pray, meditate, focus on what you're grateful for, or even engage in deep thought. For me, sitting in silence – especially meditating – was at first rather difficult, probably because I have what doctors have diagnosed as ADHD. I don't know that I agree with their diagnosis or even with the idea that ADHD is a 'disorder' (that's another conversation for another time), but I can attest that it's definitely a challenge for me to sit still and quiet my mind. Thoughts tend to race in and out, bouncing around like a pinball, almost nonstop.

So even though I would *sit* in silence, my mind didn't stop racing. The fact that sitting still and clearing my mind was so difficult for me was precisely the reason why I had to commit to mastering it. It took me three or four weeks of practising silence every day before I felt competent. I got to a place where I would allow thoughts to come in, I'd peacefully acknowledge them, and then quietly let them drift away without getting frustrated. So don't be discouraged if spending time in silence, or meditating, is at first a challenge for you.

As for how long to do your period of purposeful silence, I recommend starting with five minutes, although in the next chapter I'll teach you how you can experience the life-enhancing benefits of silence in as little as 60 seconds a day! When I began this practice, I'd sit in silence, calm and relaxed, say a prayer, meditate, ponder what I was grateful for, and just breathe deeply, for five minutes. It's such a peaceful, perfect way to start each day.

A is for Affirmations

It's the repetition of affirmations that leads to belief. Once that belief becomes a deep conviction, things begin to happen.

Muhammad Ali

You will be a failure, until you impress the subconscious with the conviction you are a success. This is done by making an affirmation which clicks.

Florence Scovel Shinn

'I am the greatest!' Muhammad Ali affirmed these words over and over again – and then he *became* them. Affirmations are one of the most effective tools for quickly becoming the person you need to be to achieve everything you want in your life. Affirmations allow you to design and then develop the mindset (thoughts, beliefs, focus) that you need to take any area of your life to the next level.

It is no coincidence that some of the most successful people in our society – celebrities like Will Smith, Jim Carrey, Suze Orman, Muhammad Ali, Oprah, and many more – have all been vocal about their belief that positive thinking and the use of affirmations has helped them on their journey to success and wealth.

Whether or not you realize it, incessantly talking to one's self is not just for crazy people. Every single one of us has an internal dialogue that runs through our heads, almost non-stop. Most of it is unconscious, that is, we don't consciously choose the dialogue. Instead, we allow our past experiences – both good and bad – to replay over and over again. Not only is this completely normal, it is one of the most important processes for each of us to learn about and master. Yet, very few people take responsibility for actively choosing to think positive, proactive thoughts that will add value to their lives.

I recently read a statistic that 80% of women have self-deprecating thoughts about themselves (body image, job performance, other people's opinion of them, etc.) throughout the day. I'm sure that men do also, although it may be to a lesser extent.

Your self-talk has dramatic influence on your level of success in every aspect of your life – confidence, health, happiness, wealth, relationships, etc. Your affirmations are either working for or against you, depending on how you are using them. If you don't consciously design and choose your affirmations you are susceptible to repeating and reliving the fears, insecurities, and limitations of your past.

However, when you actively design and write out your affirmations to be in alignment with what you want to accomplish and who you need to be to accomplish it – and commit to repeating them daily (ideally *out loud*) – they immediately make an impression on your subconscious mind. Your affirmations go to work to transform the way you think and feel so you can overcome your limiting beliefs and behaviours and replace them with those you need to succeed.

How affirmations changed my life

My first real-life exposure to the power of affirmations came when I was living with one of my most successful friends, Matt Recore. Nearly every day, I would hear Matt shouting from the shower in his bedroom. Thinking he was yelling for me, I would approach his bedroom door, only to find that he was shouting things like, 'I am in control of my destiny! I deserve to be a success! I am committed to doing everything I must do today to reach my goals and create the life of my dreams!' *What a weirdo*, I thought.

The only previous exposure I had to affirmations was through a popular 1990s spoof on the hit TV show *Saturday Night Live*, in which Al Franken's character Stuart Smalley used to stare into a mirror and repeat to himself, 'I'm good enough, I'm smart enough, and doggone it, people like me!' As a result, I always thought of affirmations as a joke. Matt knew better. As a student of Tony Robbins, Matt had been using affirmations and incantations for years to create extraordinary levels of success. Owning five homes, and one of the top network engineers in the country (all by age 25), I should have figured Matt knew what he was doing. After all, I was the one renting a room in *his* house. Unfortunately, it took me a few more years to realize that affirmations were one of the most powerful tools for trans-forming your life.

My initial first-hand experience using affirmations came when I read about them in Napoleon Hill's legendary book, *Think and Grow Rich* (which I highly recommend, by the way). Although I was skeptical that the repetition of affirmations was really going to make any measurable impact on my life, I thought I would give it a shot. If it worked for Matt, it might work for me. I chose to target the limiting belief I had devel-oped after suffering significant brain damage in my car acci-dent: *I have a horrible memory.*

If you read my first book, *Taking Life Head On!,* you know that my short-term memory was almost non-existent follow-ing my car accident. While this led to some pretty comical inci-dents, my memory was so poor that friends and family would spend hours visiting with me at the hospital, take a quick lunch break, and then return to have me greet them as if I hadn't seen them in years.

Facing such a real physical limitation due to a traumatic brain injury caused me to constantly reinforce the belief that *I have a horrible memory.* Anytime someone asked me to remem-ber or remind them of something, I would always respond, 'I would, but I really can't – I have brain damage and a horrible short-term memory.'

It had been seven years since my car accident, and while this belief was based on my reality *then*, it was time to let it go. Maybe my memory was so *horrible*, at least in part, because I had never made the effort to believe it could improve. As Henry Ford said, 'Whether you think you can, or you think you can't, you're right either way.'

If affirmations could change what was, to me, the most *justified* limiting belief that I had, then they could probably change anything. So, I created my first affirmation which read: *I let go of the limiting belief that I have a horrible memory. My brain is a miraculous organism capable of healing itself, and my memory can improve, but only in proportion to how much I believe it can improve. So, from this moment on, I am maintaining the unwavering belief that I have an excellent memory, and it's continuing to get better every day.*

I read this short affirmation every day, during my Miracle Morning. Still programmed with my past beliefs, I wasn't sure it was working. Then, two months after my first day reciting my affirmation, something occurred that hadn't occurred in over seven years. A friend asked me to remember to call her the next day, and I responded, 'Sure, no problem.' As soon as the words left my mouth, my eyes widened and I got excited! My limiting belief about my horrible memory was losing its power. I had replaced it and reprogrammed my subconscious mind with my new, empowering belief, using my affirmations.

From that point on, having also added the belief that *affirmations really work*, not only did my memory continue to improve, but I created affirmations for every area of my life that I wanted to advance. I began using affirmations to improve my health, finances, relationships, overall happiness, confidence, as well as any and all *beliefs*, *mindsets* and *habits* that needed an upgrade. Nothing was off limits. There are no limits!

How's your programming?

We've all been programmed — at the subconscious level — to think, believe, and act the way we do. Our programming is a result of many influences, including what we have been told by others, what we have told ourselves, and all of our life experiences — both good and bad. Some of us have programming that makes it easy for us to be happy and successful, while others — possibly the majority — have programming that makes life difficult.

So, the *bad news* is that if we don't actively change our programming, our potential will be crushed and our lives limited by the fears, insecurities, and limitations of our past. We must stop programming ourselves for a life of mediocrity by focusing on what we're doing wrong, being too hard on ourselves when we make mistakes, and causing ourselves to feel guilty, inadequate, and undeserving of the success we really want.

The *good news* is that our programming can be changed or improved at any time. We can reprogram ourselves to overcome all of our fears, insecurities, bad habits, and any self-limiting, potential-destroying beliefs and behaviours we currently have, so we can become as successful as we want to be, in any area of our lives we choose.

You can use affirmations to start programming yourself to be confident and successful in everything you do, simply by repeatedly telling yourself who you want to be, what you want to accomplish, and how you are going to accomplish it. With enough repetition, your subconscious mind will begin to believe what you tell it, act upon it, and eventually manifest it in your reality.

Putting your affirmations in writing makes it possible for you to choose your new programming so it moves you towards that desired condition or state of mind by enabling you to consistently review it. Constant repetition of an affirmation will lead to acceptance by the mind, and result in changes in your thoughts, beliefs and behaviours. Since you get to choose and create your affirmations, you can design them to help you establish the thoughts, beliefs and behaviours that you want and need to succeed.

Five simple steps to create your own affirmations

Here are five simple steps to create your first affirmation, followed by a link where you can download free Miracle Morning affirmations:

Step 1: What you really want

The purpose of a written affirmation is to program your mind with the beliefs, attitudes and behaviours/habits that are vital to your being able to attract, create and to sustain your ideal levels of success – Level 10 success – in every area of your life. So, your affirmation must first clearly articulate exactly what you want your ideal life to be like, in each area.

You can organize your affirmations according to the areas that you most want to focus on improving, such as health/fitness, mindset, emotions, finances, relationships, spirituality, etc. Begin with clarifying, in writing, what you really want – your ideal vision for yourself and your life – in each area.

Step 2: Why you want it

As my good friend Adam Stock, President of Rising Stock, Inc. once told me, 'The wise begin with whys'. Everyone wants to be happy, healthy, and successful, but wanting is rarely an effective strategy for getting. Those who overcome the temptations of mediocrity and achieve everything they want in life have an extraordinarily compelling *why* that drives them. They have defined a clear life purpose that is more powerful than the collective sum of their petty problems and the countless obstacles they will inevitably face, and they wake up each day and work towards their purpose.

Include why, at the deepest level, all of the things you want are important to you. Being crystal clear on your deepest *whys* will give you an unstoppable purpose.

Step 3: Who you are committed to *being* to create it

As my first coach, Jeff Sooey used to say, 'This is where the rubber meets the road'. In other words, your life gets better only *after* you get better. Your outer world improves only after you've invested countless hours improving yourself. *Being* (who you need to be) and *doing* (what you need to do) are prerequisites for *having* what you want to have. Get clear on who you need to be, are *committed* to being, in order to take your life, business, health, marriage, etc. to the next level and beyond.

Step 4: What you're committed to *doing* to attain it

Which actions will you need to take on a consistent basis to make your vision for your ideal life a reality? Want to lose weight? Your affirmation might say something like: *I am 100% committed to going to the gym five days a week and running on the treadmill for a minimum of 20 minutes.* If you're a salesperson, your affirmation might read: *I'm committed to making 20 prospecting calls every day, from 8am–9am.* The more specific your actions are, the better. Be sure to include frequency (how often), quantity (how many), and precise time frames (what times you'll begin and end your activities.)

It's also important to start small. If you're going to the gym zero days a week for zero minutes, going to five days a week for 20 minutes is a big leap. It's important to take manageable steps. Feel small successes along the way so you feel good and don't get discouraged by setting expectations too high to be able to maintain. You can build up to your ideal goal. Start by writing down a daily or weekly goal and decide when you will increase it. After a few weeks of successfully meeting your goal of going to the gym two days a week for 20 minutes, then move it up to three days a week for 20 minutes, and so on.

Step 5: Add inspirational quotes and philosophies

I am always on the lookout for quotes and philosophies that I can add to my affirmations. For example, one of my affirmations comes from the book *What Got You Here Won't Get You There* by Marshal Goldsmith. It reads: 'The #1 skill of influencers is the sincere effort to make a person feel that he or she is the most important person in the world. It's one of the skills that Bill Clinton, Oprah Winfrey, and Bruce Goodman used to become the best in their fields. I will do this for every person I connect with!'

Another reads: 'Follow Tim Ferris' advice: To maximize productivity, schedule 3–5 hour blocks or half-days of singularly focused attention on ONE single activity or project, rather than trying to switch tasks every 60 minutes.'

Any time you see or hear a quote that inspires you, or come across an empowering philosophy or strategy and think to yourself, *man, that is a huge area of improvement for me*, add it to your affirmations. By focusing on these every day, you will begin to integrate the empowering philosophies and strategies into your way of thinking and living, which will improve your results and quality of life.

Final thoughts on affirmations

- In order for your affirmations to be effective, it is important that you tap into your emotions while reading them. Mindlessly repeating a phrase over and over again, without feeling its truth, will have a minimal impact on you. You must take responsibility for generating authentic emotions and powerfully infusing those emotions into every affirmation you repeat to yourself. Have fun with it. If you're excited about an affirmation, it doesn't hurt to dance and shout it from the rooftops!
- It can also be beneficial to incorporate a purposeful *physiology*, such as reciting your affirmations while

standing tall, taking deep breaths, making a fist, or exercising. Combining physical activity with affirmations is a great way to harness the power of the mind–body connection.

- Keep in mind that your affirmations will never really be a 'final' draft, because you should always be updating them. As you continue to learn, grow and evolve, so should your affirmations. When you come up with a new goal, dream, habit or philosophy you want to integrate into your life, add it to your affirmations. When you accomplish a goal or completely integrate a new habit into your life, you might find it's no longer necessary to focus on it every day, and thus choose to remove it from your affirmations.

- Finally, you must be consistent with reading your *daily* affirmations. That's right, you must read them daily. Saying an occasional affirmation is as effective as getting an occasional workout. You won't see any measurable results until you make them a part of your daily routine. That's largely what *The Miracle Morning 30-Day Life Transformation Challenge* (in Chapter 9) is all about – making each of the *Life S.A.V.E.R.S.* a habit so you can do them effortlessly.

One more thing to consider: reading this book – or any book – is an affirmation to yourself. Anything you read influences your thoughts. When you consistently read positive self-improvement books and articles, you are programming your mind with the thoughts and beliefs that will support you in creating success.

Visit www.MiracleMorning.com/resources to:

- Get help creating and perfecting your affirmations ...
- See a sample of my own personal affirmations ...

- View and download highly effective Miracle Morning affirmations on everything from losing weight, improving your relationships, increasing your energy, developing extraordinary self-confidence, making more money, overcoming depression, and much more …

V is for Visualization

Ordinary people believe only in the possible. Extraordinary people visualize not what is possible or probable, but rather what is impossible. And by visualizing the impossible, they begin to see it as possible.

Cherie Carter-Scott

See things as you would have them be instead of as they are.

Robert Collier

Visualization, also known as *creative visualization* or *mental rehearsal*, refers to the practice of seeking to generate positive results in your outer world by using your imagination to create mental pictures of specific behaviors and outcomes occurring in your life. Frequently used by athletes to enhance their performance, visualization is the process of imagining exactly what you want to achieve or attain, and then mentally rehearsing what you'll need to do to achieve or attain it.

Many highly successful individuals, including celebrities, have advocated the use of visualization, claiming that it's played a significant role in their success. Such stars include Bill Gates, Arnold Schwarzenegger, Anthony Robbins, Tiger Woods, Will Smith, Jim Carey, and yet again, the one and only, Oprah. (Hmm ... could there be a link between Oprah being one of the most successful women in the world, and the fact that she practises most, if not *all* six of the *Life S.A.V.E.R.S.*?)

Tiger Woods, arguably the greatest golfer of all time, is famous for using visualization to mentally rehearse perfect execution of his golf swing on every hole. Another world champion golfer, Jack Nicklaus, has said: 'I never hit a shot, not even in practice, without having a very sharp in-focus picture of it in my head.'

Will Smith stated that he used visualization to overcome challenges, and visualized his success years before actually becoming successful. Another famous example is actor Jim Carrey, who wrote himself a check in 1987 in the amount of 10 million dollars. He dated it for 'Thanksgiving 1995' and added in the memo line, 'For acting services rendered'. He then visualized it for years, and in 1994 he was paid 10 million dollars for his starring role in *Dumb and Dumber*.

What do you visualize?

Most people are limited by visions of their past, replaying previous failures and heartbreaks. Creative visualization enables you to design the vision that will occupy your mind, ensuring that the greatest pull on you is your *future* – a compelling, exciting, and limitless future.

Here's a brief summary of how I use visualization, followed by three simple steps for you to create your own visualization process. After I've read my affirmations, I sit upright on my living room couch, close my eyes, and take a few slow, deep breaths. For the next five minutes, I simply visualize myself living my ideal day, performing all of my tasks with ease, confidence, and enjoyment.

For example, during the months that I spent writing this book (okay, who am I kidding – it took *years*), I would first visualize myself writing with ease, enjoying the creative process, free from stress, fear, and writer's block. I also visualized the end result – people reading the finished book, loving it and telling their friends about it. Visualizing the process being enjoyable, free from stress and fear, motivated me to take action and overcome procrastination.

Three simple steps for Miracle Morning visualization

Directly after reading your affirmations – where you took the time to articulate and focus on your goals and who you need to be to take your life to the next level – is the prime time to visualize yourself living in alignment with your affirmations.

Step 1: Get ready
Some people like to play instrumental music in the background – such as classical or baroque (check out anything from the composer Bach) – during their visualization. If

---

you'd like to experiment with playing music, put it on with the volume relatively low.

Now, sit up tall, in a comfortable position. This can be on a chair, couch, floor, etc.

Breathe deeply.

Close your eyes, clear your mind, and get ready to visualize.

Step 2: Visualize what you really want
Many people don't feel comfortable visualizing success and are even scared to succeed. Some people may experience resistance in this area. Some may even feel guilty that they will leave the other 95% behind when they become successful.

This famous quote from Marianne Williamson's book *A Return To Love*, may resonate with anyone who feels mental or emotional obstacles when attempting to visualize: 'Our deepest fear is not that we are inadequate. Our deepest fear is that we are powerful beyond measure. It is our light, not our darkness that most frightens us. We ask ourselves, who am I to be brilliant, gorgeous, talented, fabulous? Actually, who are you not to be? You are a child of God. Your playing small does not serve the world. There is nothing enlightened about shrinking so that other people won't feel insecure around you. We are all meant to shine, as children do. We were born to make manifest the glory of God that is within us. It's not just in some of us; it's in everyone. And as we let our own light shine, we unconsciously give other people permission to do the same. As we are liberated from our own fear, our presence automatically liberates others.'

The greatest gift we can give to the people we love is to live to our full potential. What does that look like for you? What do you *really* want? Forget about logic, limits, and being practical. If you could have *anything* you wanted, do anything you wanted, and be anything you wanted – what would you have? What would you do? What would you be?

Visualize your major goals, deepest desires, and most exciting, would-totally-change-my-life-if-I-achieved-them dreams. See, feel, hear, touch, taste, and smell every detail of your vision. Involve all of your senses to maximize the effectiveness of your visualization. The more vivid you make your vision, the more compelled you'll be to take the necessary actions to make it a reality.

Now, fast forward into the future to see yourself achieving your ideal outcomes and results. You can either look towards the near future – the end of the day – or further into the future, like I did while writing this book, when I visualized people reading it, loving it, and recommending it to their friends. The point is you want to see yourself accomplishing what you set out to accomplish, and you want to experience how good it will feel to have followed through and achieved your goals.

Step 3: Visualize who you need to be and what you need to do

Once you've created a clear mental picture of what you want, begin to visualize yourself living in total alignment with the person you need to be to achieve your vision. See yourself engaged in the positive actions you'll need to do each day (exercising, studying, working, writing, making calls, sending emails, etc.) and make sure you see yourself enjoying the process. See yourself smiling as you're running on that treadmill, filled with a sense of pride for your self-discipline to follow through. Picture the look of determination on your face as you confidently, persistently make those phone calls, work on that report, or finally take action and make progress on that project you've been putting off for far too long. Visualize your co-workers, customers, family, friends, and spouse responding to your positive demeanour and optimistic outlook.

Final thoughts on visualization

In addition to reading your affirmations every morning, doing this simple visualization process every day will turbo-charge the programming of your subconscious mind for success. You will begin to live in alignment with your ideal vision and make it a reality.

Visualizing your goals and dreams is believed by some experts to attract your visions into your life. Whether or not you believe in the *law of attraction*, there are practical applications for visualization. When you visualize what you want, you stir up emotions that lift your spirits and pull you towards your vision. The more vividly you see what you want, and the more intensely you allow yourself to experience *now* the feelings you will feel once you've achieved your goal, the more you make the possibility of achieving it feel real.

When you visualize daily, you align your thoughts and feelings with your vision. This makes it easier to maintain the motivation you need to continue taking the necessary actions . Visualization can be a powerful aid to overcoming self-limiting habits such as procrastination, and to taking the actions necessary to achieve your goals.

I recommend starting with just five minutes of visualization. However, in the next chapter, I'm going to teach you how you can gain the powerful benefits of visualizing in just one minute per day.

[Optional] Create your vision board

Vision boards were made popular by the bestselling book and film *The Secret* (2006). A vision board is simply a poster board on which you post images of what you want to have, who you want to become, what you want to do, where you want to live, etc.

Creating a vision board is a fun activity you can do on your own, with a friend, your significant other, or even your kids. It gives you something tangible to focus on during your visualization. If you'd like detailed instructions on this process, Christine Kane has an excellent blog on 'How to make a vision board' as well as a free eBook *The Complete Guide To Vision Boards*. Both are available on her website at www.ChristineKane.com.

Keep in mind that, although creating a vision board is fun, nothing changes in your life without action. I have to agree with Neil Farber, M.D., Ph.D., who stated in his article on psychologytoday.com, 'Vision boards are for dreaming, action boards are for achieving.' While looking at your vision board every day may increase your motivation and help you stay focused on your goals, know that only taking the necessary actions will get you real-time results.

E is for Exercise

If you don't make time for exercise, you'll probably have to make time for illness.

Robin Sharma

The only exercise most people get is jumping to conclusions, running down their friends, sidestepping responsibility, and pushing their luck.

Unknown

Morning exercise should be a staple in your daily rituals. When you exercise for even a few minutes every morning it significantly boosts your energy, enhances your health, improves self-confidence and emotional well-being, and enables you to think better and concentrate longer. Too busy for exercise? In the next chapter, I'll show you how to fit in a workout every day – in as little as *60 seconds*.

I recently saw an eye-opening video with personal development expert and self-made multi-millionaire entrepreneur, Eben Pagan, who was being interviewed by bestselling author Anthony Robbins. Tony asked, 'Eben, what is your #1 key to success?' Of course, I was very encouraged when Eben's response was, 'Start every morning off with a *personal success ritual*. That is the most important key to success.' Then he went on to talk about the importance of morning exercise.

Eben said, 'Every morning, you've got to get your heart rate up and get your blood flowing and fill your lungs with oxygen.' He continued, 'Don't just exercise at the end of the day or at the middle of the day. And even if you do like to exercise at those times, always incorporate at least 10 to 20 minutes of jumping jacks or some sort of aerobic exercise in the morning.'

The benefits of morning exercise are too many to ignore. From waking you up and enhancing your mental clarity, to helping you sustain higher levels of energy throughout the day, exercising soon after rising can improve your life in many ways.

Whether you go to the gym, go for a walk or run, throw on a P90X or *Insanity* DVD, what you do during your period of exercise is up to you, although I'll share some recommendations.

Personally, if I were only allowed to practise one form of exercise for the rest of my life, I would, without a doubt choose yoga. I began practising yoga shortly after I created *The Miracle Morning*, and have been doing it – and loving it – ever since. It's such a complete form of exercise, as it combines *stretching* with *strength training* with *cardio* with *focused breathing*, and can even be a form of *meditation*.

Meet the one and only ... *Dashama*

I can't talk about yoga (or exercise for that matter) without talking about my friend Dashama. A few years ago, one of her students introduced me to her work as one of the world's leading yoga instructors. Dashama is the most authentic, spiritual, practical and all-around most effective yoga teacher I have ever come across. I asked her to share her unique perspective on the benefits of yoga.

From Dashama: 'Yoga is a multi-faceted science that has applications for the physical, mental, emotional and spiritual aspects of life. That being said, when Hal asked me to contribute a short introduction to yoga, for this book, I felt it was in perfect alignment with *The Miracle Morning*. I know from personal experience that yoga can help you create miracles in your life. I've experienced it in mine and also witnessed it in countless others whom I have taught around the world.

The important thing to remember is that yoga can take place in many forms. Whether it is sitting in silent meditation, breathing to expand your lung capacity or back bending to open your heart – there are practices that can help every aspect of your life. The key is to learn which techniques to practise when you need a remedy and use it to your advantage to bring yourself into balance.

A well-rounded yoga practice can enhance your life in so many ways. It can heal what is out of harmony and can move stuck or blocked energy through your body, creating space for new fluid movement, blood flow and energy to circulate. I encourage you to listen to your body and try some new sequences as you feel ready. To learn more and see instructional yoga videos, feel free to visit my website at pranashama.com.

Blessings and Love, Dashama

Final thoughts on exercise

You know that if you want to maintain good health and increase your energy, you must exercise consistently. That's not news to anybody. But it's too easy to make excuses as to why we don't exercise. Two of the biggest are 'I just don't have time' and 'I'm just too tired'. There is no limit to the excuses that you can think of. The more creative you are the more excuses you can come up with, right?

That's the beauty of incorporating exercise into your Miracle Morning; it happens before your day wears you out, before you have a chance to get too tired, before you have an entire day to come up with new excuses for avoiding exercise. *The Miracle Morning* is really a sure fire way to avoid all of those excuses, and to make exercise a daily habit. (More on the easy way to implement positive habits into your life, like exercise, in Chapter 9 which will enhance your quality of life for years to come.)

Legal disclaimer: Hopefully this goes without saying, but you should consult your doctor or physician before beginning any exercise regimen, especially if you are experiencing any physical pain, discomfort, disabilities, etc. You may need to modify or even refrain from your exercise routine to meet your individual needs.

R is for Reading

A person who won't read has no advantage over one
who can't read.

Mark Twain

Reading is to the mind what exercise is to the body and prayer
is to the soul. We become the books we read.

Matthew Kelly

Reading, the fifth practice in the *Life S.A.V.E.R.S.*, is the fast track to transforming any area of your life. It is one of the most immediate methods for acquiring the knowledge, ideas, and strategies you need to achieve Level 10 success in any area of your life.

The key is to learn from the experts – those who have already done what you want to do. Don't reinvent the wheel. The fastest way to achieve everything you want is to model successful people who have already achieved it. With an almost infinite amount of books available on every topic, there are no limits to the knowledge you can gain through daily reading.

I recently heard someone say in a mocking, *I'm too cool for this* tone, 'Uh, yeah, I don't read 'self-help' books,' as if such books were beneath him. Poor guy. I'm not sure if it's his ego or just lack of awareness, but he's missing out on the unlimited supply of knowledge, boundless growth, and life-changing ideas he could gain from some of the most brilliant, successful individuals in the world. Who in their right mind would choose not to do that?

Whatever you want for your life, there are countless books on how to get it. Want to become wealthy, rich, a multi-millionaire? There are plenty of books written by those who have achieved the pinnacles of financial success which will teach you how. Here are a few of my favourites (full details are given at the back of the book):

- *The Millionaire Fastlane* by MJ DeMarco
- *Think and Grow Rich* by Napoleon Hill
- *Secrets of the Millionaire Mind* by T. Harv Eker
- *Total Money Makeover* by Dave Ramsey

Want to create an incredible, loving, supportive and romantic relationship? There are probably more books on how to do exactly that than you could read in a decade. Here are a few of my favourites:

- *The Five Love Languages* by Gary D. Chapman
- *The SoulMate Experience* by Jo Dunn
- *The Seven Principles For Making a Marriage Work* by John M. Gottman and Nan Silver

Whether you'd like to transform your relationships, increase your self-confidence, improve your communication or persuasion skills, learn how to become wealthy, or improve any area of your life, head to your local bookstore – or do what I do and head to Amazon.com – and you'll find a plethora of books on any area of your life you want to improve. For those who want to minimize our carbon footprint or save money, I also recommend utilizing your local library or checking out one of my favorite websites, www.paperbackswap.com.

For a complete list of my favourite personal development books – including those that have made the biggest impact on my success and happiness – check out the Recommended Reading list located at www.MiracleMorning.com/resources.

How much should you read?

I recommend making a commitment to read a minimum of ten pages per day (although five is okay to start with, if you read slowly or don't yet enjoy reading). Let's do some maths on this for a second: reading ten pages read per day is not going to break you, but it will *make* you. We're only talking 10–15 minutes of reading, or 15–30 minutes if you read more slowly.

Look at it this way. If you quantify that, reading just ten pages a day will average 3650 pages a year, which equates to approximately eighteen 200-page personal development/self-improvement books! Let me ask you, if you read 18 personal development books in the next 12 months, do you think you will be more knowledgeable, capable and confident – a new and improved *you*? Absolutely!

Final thoughts on reading

- Begin with the end in mind. Before you begin reading each day, ask yourself why you are reading that book – what do you want to gain from it – and keep that outcome in mind. Take a moment to do this now by asking yourself what you want to gain from reading this book. Are you committed to finishing it? More importantly, are you committed to implementing what you're learning and taking action, by following through with *The Miracle Morning 30-Day Life Transformation Challenge* at the end?
- Many Miracle Morning practitioners use their reading time to catch up on their religious texts, such as the Bible, Torah, or any other spiritual text.
- Hopefully you took the advice I gave and you've been underlining, circling, highlighting, folding the corners of pages, and taking notes in the margins of this book. To get the most out of any book I read and make it easy for me to revisit the content again in the future, I underline or circle anything that I may want to re-visit, and make notes in the margins to remind me why I underlined that particular section. (Unless, of course, it's a library book). This process of marking books as I read allows me to come back at any time and recapture all of the key lessons, ideas, and benefits without needing to read the book again, cover to cover.
- I highly recommend re-reading good personal development books. Rarely can we read a book once and internalize all of the value from that book. Achieving mastery in any area requires repetition – being exposed to certain ideas, strategies, or techniques over and over again, until they become engrained in your subconscious mind. For example,

if you wanted to master karate, you wouldn't learn the techniques once and then think, 'I got this'. No, you'd learn the techniques, practise them, then go back to your sensei and learn them again, and repeat the process hundreds of times in order to master a single technique. Mastering techniques to improve your life works the same way. There is more value in re-reading a book you already know has strategies that can improve your life than there is in reading a new book before you've mastered the strategies in the first. Whenever I'm reading a book that I see can really make an impact on an area of my life, I commit to re-reading that book (or at least re- reading the parts I've underlined, circled and highlighted) as soon as I'm finished going through it the first time. I actually keep a special space on my bookshelf for the books that I want to re- read. I've read books like *Think and Grow Rich* as many as three times, and often refer back to them throughout the year. Re-reading requires discipline, because it is typically more 'fun' to read a book you've never read before. Repetition can be boring or tedious (which is why so few people ever 'master' anything), but that's even more reason why we should do it – to develop a higher level of self-discipline. Why not try it out with this book? Commit to re-reading it as soon as you're finished, to deepen your learning and give yourself more time to master *The Miracle Morning*.

S is for Scribing

Whatever it is that you write, putting words on the page is a
form of therapy that doesn't cost a dime.

Diana Raab

Ideas can come from anywhere and at any time. The problem
with making mental notes is that the ink fades very rapidly.

Rolf Smith

Scribing is the final practice in the *Life S.A.V.E.R.S.* and is really just another word for *writing*, but please allow me to keep it real – I needed an 'S' for the end of Life S.A.V.E.R.S. because a 'W' wouldn't fit anywhere. Thanks thesaurus, I owe you one.

Journaling

My favourite form of scribing is journaling, which I do for 5–10 minutes during my Miracle Morning. By getting your thoughts out of your head and putting them in writing, you gain valuable insights you'd otherwise never see. The scribing element of your Miracle Morning enables you to document your insights, ideas, breakthroughs, realizations, successes and lessons learned, as well as any areas of opportunity, personal growth, or improvement.

While I had known about the profound benefits of journaling for years – and I had even tried it a few times – I never stuck with it consistently, because it was never part of my daily routine. Usually, I kept a journal by my bed, and when I'd get home late at night, nine times out of ten I would find myself making the excuse that I was too tired to write in it. My journals stayed mostly blank. Even though I already had many mostly blank journals sitting on my bookshelf, every so often I would buy myself a brand new journal – a more expensive one – convincing myself that if I spent a lot of money on it, I would surely write in it. Seems like a decent theory, right? Unfortunately, my little strategy never worked, and for years I just accumulated more and more increasingly expensive, yet equally empty journals.

That was before *The Miracle Morning*. From day one, *The Miracle Morning* gave me the time and structure to write in my journal *every day*, and it quickly became one of my favourite habits. I can tell you now that journaling has become one of the most gratifying and fulfilling practices of my life. Not only do I derive the daily benefits of consciously directing my thoughts and putting them in writing, but even more powerful are those I have gained from reviewing my journals, from cover to cover, afterwards – especially, at the end of the year. It is hard to put into words how overwhelmingly constructive the experience of going back and reviewing your journals can be, but I'll do my best.

MY FIRST JOURNAL REVIEW

On 31 December, after my first year doing *The Miracle Morning* and writing in my journal, I began reading the first page I had written that year. Day by day, I started to review and *relive* my entire year. I was able to revisit my mindset from each day, and gain a new perspective as to how much I had grown throughout the year. I re-examined my actions, activities and progress, giving me a new appreciation for how much I had accomplished during the past 12 months. Most importantly, I recaptured the lessons I had learned, many of which I had forgotten over the course of the year.

Gratitude 2.0: I also experienced a much deeper quality of gratitude – in a way that I had never experienced before – on two different levels, simultaneously. It was what I now refer to as my first *Back to the Future* moment. Try to follow me here (and feel free to picture me as Marty McFly stepping out of a 1985 DeLorean). As I read through my journal, my current self (which was also the *future* self of who I was at the time I wrote those journal entries) was now looking back at all of the people, experiences, lessons and accomplishments that I took note of being grateful for throughout the year. As I was in that moment reliving the gratitude that I felt in the past, I was simultaneously feeling grateful in the present moment for how far I had come since that time in my life. It was a remarkable experience, and a bit surreal.

Accelerated growth: Then, I began to tap into the highest point of value I would gain from reviewing my journals. I pulled out a sheet of blank paper, drew a line down the middle, and wrote two headings at the top: *Lessons Learned and New Commitments*. As I read through my hundreds of my journal entries, I found myself recapturing dozens of valuable lessons.

This process of recapturing *Lessons Learned* and making *New Commitments* to implement those lessons aided my personal growth and development more than almost anything else.

While there are many worthwhile benefits of keeping a daily journal, a few of which I've just described, here are a few more of my favourites:

- **Gain clarity:** The process of writing something down forces us to think through it enough to understand it. Journaling will give you more clarity, allow you to brainstorm, and help you work through problems.
- **Capture ideas:** Journaling helps you not only expand your ideas, but also prevents you from losing the important ideas that you may want to act on in the future.
- **Review lessons:** It enables you to review all of the lessons you've learned.
- **Acknowledge your progress:** It's wonderful to go back and re-read your journal entries from a year ago and see how much progress you've made. It's one of the most empowering, confidence-inspiring and enjoyable experiences. It can't really be duplicated any other way.

Gap Focus: Is it hurting or helping you?

In the opening pages of this chapter, we talked about using the *Life S.A.V.E.R.S.* to close your 'potential gap'. Human beings are conditioned to have what I call *gap focus*. We tend to focus on the gaps between where we are in life and where we want to be, between what we've accomplished and what we could have or want to accomplish, and the gap between who we are and our idealistic vision of the person we believe we should be.

The problem with this is that constant 'gap focus' can be detrimental to our confidence and self-image, causing us to feel like we don't have enough, haven't accomplished enough, and that we're simply not good enough, or at least, not as good as we should be.

High achievers are typically the worst at this, constantly overlooking or minimizing their accomplishments, beating themselves up over every mistake and imperfection, and never feeling like anything they do is quite good enough.

The irony is that 'gap focus' is a big part of the reason that high achievers *are* high achievers. Their insatiable desire to close the gap is what fuels their pursuit of excellence and constantly drives them to achieve. 'Gap focus' can be healthy and productive if it comes from a positive, proactive, *I'm committed to and excited about fulfilling my potential* perspective, without any feelings of lack. Unfortunately, it rarely does. The average person, even the average high achiever, tends to focus negatively on their gaps.

The *highest* achievers – those who are balanced and focused on achieving Level 10 success in nearly every area of their lives – are exceedingly grateful for what they have, regularly acknowledge themselves for what they've accomplished, and are always at peace with where they are in their lives. It's the dueling idea that *I am doing the best that I can in this moment, and at the same time, I can and will do better*. This balanced self-assessment prevents that feeling of lack – of not being, having, doing enough – while still allowing them to constantly strive to close their potential gap in each area.

Typically, when a day, week, month, or year ends, and we're in 'gap focus' mode, it's almost impossible to maintain an accurate assessment of ourselves and our progress. For example, if you had ten things on your to-do list for the day – even if you completed six of them – your 'gap focus' causes you to feel you didn't get everything done that you wanted to do.

The majority of people do dozens, even hundreds, of things *right* during the day, and a few things wrong. Guess which things people remember and replay in their minds over and over again? Doesn't it make more sense to focus on the 100 things you did right? It sure is more enjoyable.

What does this have to do with writing in a journal? Writing in a journal each day, with a *structured*, strategic process (more on that in a minute) allows you to direct your focus to what you did accomplish, what you're grateful for, and what you're committed to doing better tomorrow. Thus, you more deeply enjoy your journey each day, feel good about any forward progress you made, and use a heightened level of clarity to accelerate your results.

Effective journaling

Here are three simple steps to get started with journaling, or improve your current journaling process.

1 **Choose a format – digital or traditional:** You'll want to decide up front if you want to go with a traditional, physical lined journal, or go with a digital journal (such as on your computer, or an app for your phone or tablet). Having used both traditional and digital, there are advantages and disadvantages to both formats (which I'll address in a minute), but it really comes down to your personal preference. Do you prefer to write by hand, or would you rather type your daily journal entries? That should make it a relatively simple decision as to which format to use.

2 **Get a journal:** When it comes to a *traditional* journal, while just about anything can work (you can even use

a cheap spiral notebook), since you're probably going to have it for the rest of your life there is something to be said about getting a nice, durable journal that you enjoy looking at. Get a journal that is not only lined, but also dated, with room to write for all 365 days of the year. I've found that having a pre-designated (dated) space to write keeps me accountable to follow through each day, since I can't help but notice when I miss a day or two, because they're blank. This usually motivates me to go back and mentally review those missed days and catch up my journal entries. It's also nice to have dated journals for every year, so you can easily go back and review any time in your life (and experience those benefits I described above in 'My first journal review'. One of my favorite lined, dated journals is 'The Winners Journal' (www.TheWinnersJournal.com), which I used from 2007–9, and was very pleased with the results. In fact, it's what inspired me to design and create *The Miracle Morning Journal* (which is now available on Amazon.com). You can even download a free sample of *The Miracle Morning Journal* at the website given below.

If you prefer to use a digital journal, there are also many choices available. My favourite journaling app is 'Five-Minute Journal' (available at www.FiveMinute-Journal.com) and is becoming very popular. It makes it easy by giving you prompts, such as 'I am grateful for ...' and 'What would make today great?' It takes only five minutes or less, and includes an 'Evening' option, which allows you to review your day and even upload photos to create visual memories.

Again, it really comes down to your preference and which features you want. Just type 'online journal' into Google or 'journal' into the App Store, and you'll get a variety of choices.

3 **Decide what to write:** There are infinite aspects of your life that you can journal about, and countless types of journals. Gratitude journals, dream journals, food journals, workout journals, etc. You can write about your goals, dreams, plans, family, commitments, lessons learned, and anything else that you feel you need to focus on in your life. My journaling method ranges from being a very specific, structured process – *listing what I'm grateful for, acknowledging my accomplishments, clarifying what areas I want to improve on, and planning which specific actions I'm committed to taking to improve* – to being pretty traditional, just a dated entry with a synopsis of my day. I find both to be very valuable, and it's nice to mix it up.

To get a free sample of *The Miracle Morning Journal*, go to www.MiracleMorning.com/resources.

Do you want to write a book?

According to a survey done by *USA Today*, 82% of Americans want to write a book, but the #1 obstacle preventing them? You guessed it – they can't find the *time*. If you have ever wanted to write a book, you can use your Miracle Morning time to do just that. In fact, right now I am writing this to you at 6.03 am, during my Miracle Morning.

I believe that everyone has a book inside of them containing their own unique value to offer to the world. In fact, I've recently started coaching many of my private clients on how to start (or finish) their first (or next) book, and how to write a book that not only becomes a bestseller (that's the easy part), but a book that creates a movement.

I'm always excited to hear people's stories and what they're passionate to write – I mean, *scribe* – about.

Customizing the Life S.A.V.E.R.S.

In Chapter 8, you'll learn how you can personalize and customize nearly every aspect of your Miracle Morning to fit your lifestyle. For now, I want to share a few ideas specifically towards customizing the *Life S.A.V.E.R.S.* based on your schedule and preferences. Your current morning routine might only allow you to fit in a 20- or 30-minute Miracle Morning, or you might choose to do a longer version on the weekends.

Here is an example of a fairly common, 60-minute Miracle Morning schedule, using the *Life S.A.V.E.R.S.*

The Miracle Morning (60-minute) sample schedule:

Using the *Life S.A.V.E.R.S.*

- Silence (5 minutes)
- Affirmations (5 minutes)
- Visualization (5 minutes)
- Exercise (20 minutes)
- Reading (20 minutes)
- Scribing (5 minutes)

Total time: 60 minutes

The sequence in which you do the *Life S.A.V.E.R.S.* can also be customized to your preferences. Some people prefer to do their *exercise* first, as a way to increase their blood flow and wake themselves up. However, you might prefer to do *exercise* as your last activity in the *Life S.A.V.E.R.S.* so you're not sweaty during your Miracle Morning. Personally, I prefer to start with a period of peaceful, purposeful *silence* – so that I can wake up slowly, clear my mind, and focus my energy and intentions. I save *exercise* for my last activity, that way I can jump directly into the shower and proceed with the rest of my day. However, this is your Miracle Morning – not mine – so feel free to experiment with different sequences and see which you like best.

Final thoughts on the Life S.A.V.E.R.S.

Everything is difficult before it's easy. Every new experience is uncomfortable before it's comfortable. The more you practise the *Life S.A.V.E.R.S.* the more natural and normal each of them will feel. Remember that my first time meditating was almost my last, as my mind raced like a Ferrari and my thoughts bounced around uncontrollably like the silver sphere in a pinball machine. Now, I love meditation, and while I'm no *master*, I'd say I'm decent at it. Similarly, my first time doing yoga, I felt like a fish out of water. I wasn't flexible, couldn't do the poses correctly, and felt awkward and uncomfortable. Now, yoga is my favourite form of exercise, and I am so grateful that I stuck with it.

I invite you to begin practising the *Life S.A.V.E.R.S.* now, so you can become familiar and comfortable with each of them, and get a jump-start before you begin *The Miracle Morning 30-Day Life Transformation Challenge* (in Chapter 10). If your biggest concern is still *finding time*, don't worry, I've got you covered. In the next chapter, you're going to learn how to do the entire Miracle Morning – receiving the full benefits from all six of the *Life S.A.V.E.R.S.* – in only six minutes a day.

7

The six-minute Miracle Morning (real results in six minutes)

On the one hand, we all want to be happy. On the other hand, we all know the things that make us happy. But we don't do those things. Why? Simple. We are too busy. Too busy doing what? Too busy trying to be happy.

Matthew Kelly

I don't have time to wake up early.

Unknown

Oh, you're busy? Weird. I thought it was just me.

Probably the most common question – or concern – I get about *The Miracle Morning* is regarding *how long* it needs to be. When I first had the breakthrough realization about how our levels of success (and fulfilling our potential) in every area of life are being limited by our insufficient (or non-existent) level of personal development, my biggest challenge was *finding time* to act on this realization.

As I've developed and shared *The Miracle Morning* over the years, I've been very aware of the need to make it scalable so that even the busiest among us can make time for our Miracle Morning. I developed the 'six-minute Miracle Morning' for those days when you're extra busy and pressed for time, as well as for those of you who are so overwhelmed with your life situation right now that just thinking about adding *one more thing* stresses you out.

I think we can all agree that investing a minimum of six minutes into becoming the person we need to be to create the levels of success and happiness we truly want in our lives is not only reasonable, it's an absolute must, even when we're pressed for time. I think you will be pleasantly surprised in the next few minutes as you read and realize how *powerful* (and life-changing) these six minutes can be!

Imagine if the first six minutes of every morning began like this ...

- **Minute One...** Envision yourself waking up peacefully in the morning, with a big yawn, a stretch, and a smile on your face. Instead of rushing carelessly into your hectic day – stressed and overwhelmed – you spend the first minute sitting quietly, in purposeful *silence*. You sit, very calm, very peaceful, and breathe deeply, slowly. Maybe you say a prayer of gratitude to appreciate the moment, or pray for guidance on your journey. Maybe you decide to try your first minute of meditation. As you sit in silence, you're totally present in the now, in the moment. You calm your mind, relax your body, and allow all of your stress to melt away. You develop a deeper sense of peace, purpose, and direction ...

- **Minute Two...** You pull out your daily *affirmations* – the ones that remind you of your unlimited potential and your most important priorities – and you read them out loud from top to bottom. As you focus on what's most important to you, your level of internal motivation increases. Reading over the reminders of how capable you *really* are gives you a feeling of confidence. Looking over what you're committed to, what your purpose is, and what your goals are re-energizes you to take the actions necessary to *live* the life you truly want, deserve, and now *know* is possible for you...

- **Minute Three...** You close your eyes, or you look at your vision board, and you visualize. Your visualization could include what it will look and feel like when you reach your goals. You visualize the day going perfectly, see yourself enjoying your work, smiling and laughing with your family or your significant other, and easily accomplishing all that you intend to accomplish for that day. You see what it will look like, you feel what it will feel like, and you experience the joy of what you will create...

- **Minute Four...** You take one minute to write down some of the things that you're grateful for, what you're proud of, and the results you're committed to creating for that day. In doing so, you create for yourself an empowered, inspired, and confident state of mind...

- **Minute Five...** Then, you grab your self-help book and invest one miraculous minute reading a page or two. You learn a new idea, something you can incorporate into your day which will improve your results at work or in your relationships. You discover something new that you can use to think and feel better – to *live* better...

- **Minute Six...** Finally, you stand up and spend the last minute moving your body for 60 seconds. Maybe you run in place, maybe you do a minute of jumping-jacks. Maybe you do push-ups or sit-ups. The point is that you're getting your heart rate up, generating energy and increasing your ability to be alert and focused.

How would you feel if that's how you utilized the first six minutes of each day? How would the quality of your day – your life – improve?

I don't suggest you limit your Miracle Morning to only six minutes every day, but as I said, on those days when you're pressed for time, the six-minute Miracle Morning provides a powerful strategy for accelerating your personal development.

8

Customizing your Miracle Morning to fit your lifestyle and achieve your biggest goals and dreams

The Miracle Morning is amazing. It has provided new levels of clarity, focus, and energy to my life. What's great is that it can be a different routine for each person, depending on your goals and schedule. For me, as a business owner and mother of a one-year-old, it has been a time to reflect, pray, focus on my goals and dreams, exercise, and de-stress. It also gives me valuable time to be thankful for the people, events, and blessings in my life. We all have the same 168 hours in a week; so start using *The Miracle Morning* and you'll find miracles in your life that you never knew existed!

Katie Heaney, owner, Hedgehog Group
(Saint Louis, MO)

Up until this point, we've primarily been focused on the *Life S.A.V.E.R.S.* model to accelerate your personal development during your Miracle Morning. However, *The Miracle Morning* is 100% customizable. Everything from your wake-up time to the total duration of your Miracle Morning to which activities you do, as well as the duration and order of each activity – there is no limit to how your Miracle Morning can be personalized to fit your lifestyle and help you achieve your most significant goals, faster than ever before.

Here I'll cover all of the above, as well as when (and what) to eat in the morning, how to align *The Miracle Morning* with your major goals and dreams, what to do on the weekends, a tip on overcoming procrastination, and much more.

Wake-up and start time

This may sound completely counter intuitive, but stick with me. You don't actually have to do *The Miracle Morning* in the *morning*.

Huh?

Of course there are undeniable advantages to early rising and getting a proactive start to your day. However, for some, their unique schedule and lifestyle simply may not allow it. Obviously, someone who works the graveyard shift, or even late-nights, is going to have a different wake up time than someone who is in bed by 9.00 pm every evening. Considering that different people have different schedules, the essence of *The Miracle Morning* remains that you simply wake up *earlier* than you normally would (typically by 30–60 minutes), so that you can dedicate time every day to improving yourself, so you can transform your life.

When, why and what to eat (in the morning)

Up until this point, you may have been wondering *when do I get to eat during my Miracle Morning?!* I'll cover that here. Besides *when* you eat during your Miracle Morning, *what* you choose to eat is even more critical, and *why* you choose to eat what you eat may be most important of all.

When to eat

Keep in mind that digesting food is one of the most energy-draining processes the body goes through each day. The bigger the meal, the more food you give your body to digest, the more drained you will feel. With that in mind, I recommend eating *after* your Miracle Morning. This ensures that, for optimum alertness and focus during the *Life S.A.V.E.R.S.*, your blood will be flowing to your brain rather than to your stomach to digest your food.

If you feel like you must eat something first thing in the morning, make sure that it's a small, light, easily digestible meal, such as fresh fruit or a smoothie (more on that in a minute).

Why to eat

Let's take a moment to discuss *why* you eat the foods that you do. When you're shopping at the grocery store, or selecting food from a menu at a restaurant, what criteria do you use to determine which foods you are going to put into your body? Are your choices based purely on taste? Texture? Convenience? Are they based on health? Energy? Dietary restrictions?

Most people eat the foods they do based mainly on the taste, and at a deeper level, based on our emotional attachment to the foods we like the taste of. If you were to ask someone, 'Why did you eat that ice cream? Why did you drink that fizzy drink?' Or, 'Why did you bring that fried chicken home from the supermarket?' You would most likely hear responses like, 'Mmm, because I love ice cream! I like drinking fizzy drinks. I was in the mood for fried chicken.' All answers based on the emotional enjoyment derived primarily from the way these foods taste. In this case, this person is not likely to explain their food choices with how much value these foods will add to their health, or how much sustained energy they'll get.

My point is this: If we want to have more energy (which we all do) and if we want our lives to be healthy and disease-free (which we all do) then it's crucial that we re-examine why we eat the foods that we do, and – this is important – *start valuing the health benefits and energy consequences of the foods we eat as much as or more than the taste.* In no way am I saying that we should eat foods that don't taste good in exchange for the health and energy benefits. I'm saying that we can have both. I'm saying that if we want to live every day with an abundance of energy so we can perform at our best and live a long, healthy life, we must choose to eat more foods that are good for our health and give us sustained energy, as well as tasting great.

What to eat

Before we talk about what to eat, let's take a second to talk about what to *drink*. Remember that Step 4 of the five-step snooze-proof wake-up strategy (Chapter 10) is to drink a full glass of water – first thing in the morning – so you can rehydrate and reenergize after a full night of sleep. Next, I typically start my Miracle Morning by brewing a cup of Bulletproof Coffee. I actually set my alarm 15 minutes earlier each day, to give myself time to make my coffee without intruding on my Miracle Morning time.

As for what to eat, it has been proven that a diet rich in *living* foods, such as fresh fruits and vegetables will greatly increase your energy levels, improve your mental focus and emotional wellbeing, keep you healthy, and protect you from disease. So, I created *The Miracle Morning* super-food smoothie that incorporates everything your body needs in one tall, frosty glass! I'm talking about complete protein (*all* of the essential amino acids), age-defying antioxidants, Omega 3 essential fatty acids (to boost immunity, cardio-vascular health, and brain power), plus a rich spectrum of vitamins and minerals ... and that's just for starters. I haven't even mentioned all the super-foods, such as the stimulating, mood-lifting phytonutrients in Cacao (the tropical bean from which chocolate is made), the long-lasting energy of Maca (the Andean adaptogen revered for its hormone-balancing effects), and the immune-boosting nutrients and appetite-suppressing properties of Chia seeds.

The Miracle Morning super-food smoothie not only pro-vides you with sustained energy, it also tastes great. You might even find that it enhances your ability to create mir-acles in your everyday life. You can get the recipe free at www.MiracleMorning.com/resources.

Remember the old saying, 'You are what you eat'? Take care of your body so your body will take care of you. You will feel vibrant energy and enhanced clarity immediately!

Aligning The Miracle Morning
with your goals and dreams

Most Miracle Morning practitioners and high achievers use their daily practice to enhance their focus on their immedi-ate goals and their most significant dreams. This is especially true for those they've been putting off, or haven't been making time for – such as starting a business or writing a book. The *Life S.A.V.E.R.S.* are ideal for improving your ability to stay focused on your goals and accelerating the rate at which you make progress towards your dreams.

For example, when you create your *affirmations*, make sure that they are in alignment with your goals and dreams, and that they clarify what you will need to think, believe and do to achieve them, so they reinforce your unwavering commitment to follow through. Reading them daily will keep you focused on your highest priorities and the steps you need to take to achieve them.

When you are doing your morning *visualization*, visualize yourself effortlessly enjoying the process of achieving your goals (like I did while writing this book) and keep a clear picture of what it will look like once achieved. Remember to involve all of your senses – see, feel, taste, touch, and even smell every detail of your vision and your ideal outcomes. The more vivid your vision is, the more effective it will be in increasing your desire and motivation to take the necessary steps towards your goals each day.

Overcoming procrastination: do the worst, first

One of the most effective strategies for overcoming habitual procrastination and maximizing your productivity is to start working on your most important – or *least enjoyable* – tasks, first thing in the morning.

In his bestselling book *Eat That Frog!*, the legendary productivity expert Brian Tracy shows how getting things done in the morning leads to mental rewards that can take us to great heights in our lives. It is the idea that doing the hard task first ('frog eating') and getting it out of the way creates momentum and makes the rest of the day more productive.

The purpose of *The Miracle Morning* is more about waking up *with purpose* – combining the benefits of early rising and personal development – and isn't so much concerned with which activities you do, as long as the activities you choose are proactive and help you improve your inner world (yourself) and your outer world (your life).

In this short chapter I'll give you some ideas and strategies for how you can design your Miracle Morning and adjust it to fit your lifestyle so it adds value to your life and helps you achieve your most important goals. I'll also include examples of different real-life Miracle Mornings, designed by individuals – from entrepreneurs to stay-at-home moms, to high school and college students – to fit their unique schedules, priorities, and lifestyles.

The Miracle Morning *on weekends*

Waking up early on Saturday gives me an edge in finishing my work with a very relaxed state of mind. There is a feeling of time pressure on weekdays that aren't there on weekends. If I wake up early in the morning, before anybody else, I can plan the day or at least my activities with relaxed mind.

Oprah Winfrey

I couldn't agree with Oprah more. When I first created *The Miracle Morning* I only did it Monday through Friday, and I took the weekends off. It didn't take long for me to realize that every day I did *The Miracle Morning* I felt better, more fulfilled and more productive, but every day that I slept in, I woke feeling lethargic, unfocused, and unproductive.

Experiment for yourself. You may start, as I did, by doing *The Miracle Morning* during the week and try taking the weekends off. See how you feel on those Saturday and Sunday mornings, sleeping in. If you feel, like many people do, that *every day* is better when you begin it with The Miracle Morning, you might just find that weekends are actually your favourite time to do it.

Keeping your Miracle Morning fresh, fun and exciting!

Over the years, my Miracle Morning continues to evolve. While I still practise the *Life S.A.VE.R.S.* daily and don't foresee any reason I would ever stop needing the benefits of those six practices, I do think it's important to mix things up and keep variety in your Miracle Morning. Like a relationship, you always want to keep a little fun and excitement in the mix, so things don't get boring or stale.

For example, you might change up your morning exercise routine every 90 days, or even monthly. You could try different meditations, either through a simple Google search or by downloading various meditation apps on your phone. You could create a vision board and update it regularly. As I mentioned during the section on affirmations: you should always be updating your affirmations to stimulate your senses and to be in alignment with your always-evolving vision for who you can and want to be.

I also adjust my Miracle Morning on the fly, based on my changing schedule, circumstances, and projects I'm working on. When I'm preparing for an upcoming speech or seminar that I'll be presenting, I allocate more time during my Miracle Morning to practise and rehearse my performance. When I'm travelling, to give speeches for colleges or corporations, and I'm staying in hotels, I adjust my Miracle Morning accordingly. For example, if I'm scheduled to give a late night keynote or workshop at a conference, I will move my wake up and start time a little later.

Another example of making adjustments based on my current projects has been during this past few months, as my Miracle Morning has ironically been heavily focused on completing this book. I've still maintained the *Life S.A.VE.R.S.* – I've just done a shortened version, so I can focus more of my time on writing.

As you can see, you can always design and customize *The Miracle Morning* to fit *your* lifestyle.

Final thoughts on customizing your Miracle Morning

Humans need variety. It's important that you keep your Miracle Morning feeling fresh and new. As one of my first mentors once told me whenever I complained about my work as a sales rep getting boring, 'Whose fault is it that it's boring? And whose responsibility is it to make it fun again?' This is a great lesson that I've never forgotten. Whether it's our routines or our relationships, it's our responsibility to actively and continuously make them the way we want them to be.

Remember, the moment you accept total responsibility for *everything* in your life is the moment you claim the power to change *anything* in your life.

9

From unbearable to unstoppable: The real secret to forming habits that will transform your life (in 30 days)

Successful people aren't born that way. They become successful by establishing the habit of doing things unsuccessful people don't like to do. The successful people don't always like doing these things themselves; they just get on and do them.

Don Marquis

Motivation is what gets you started. Habit is what keeps you going.

Jim Rohn

It's been said that our quality of life is created by the quality of our habits. If a person is living a successful life, then that person simply has the habits in place that are creating and sustaining their levels of success. On the other hand, if someone is not experiencing the levels of success they want – no matter what the area – they simply haven't committed to putting the necessary habits in place which will create the results they want.

Considering that our habits create our life, there is arguably no single *skill* that is more important for you to learn and master than controlling your habits. You must identify, implement, and maintain the habits necessary for creating the results you want in your life, while learning how to let go of any negative habits which are holding you back from achieving your true potential.

Habits are behaviours that are repeated regularly and tend to occur subconsciously. Whether you realize it or not, your life has been, and will continue to be, created by your habits. If you don't control your habits, your habits will control you.

Unfortunately, if you're like the rest of us, you were never taught how to successfully implement and sustain (aka 'master') positive habits. There's no class offered in school called 'Habit Mastery'. There should be. Such a course would probably be more important to your success and overall quality of life than all of the other courses combined.

Because they never learned to master their habits, most people fail at virtually every attempt to control them, time and time again. Take New Year's resolutions, for example.

Habitual failure: New Year's Resolutions (NYRs)

Every year, millions of well-intentioned people make New Year's resolutions, but less than 5% of us stick to them. A NYR is really just a *positive* habit (like exercising or early rising) you want to incorporate into your life, or a *negative* habit (like smoking or eating fast food) you want to get rid of. You don't need a statistic to tell you that, when it comes to NYRs, most people have already given up and thrown in the towel before January has even come to a close.

Maybe you've seen this phenomenon in real time. If you've ever gone to the gym the first week of January, you know how difficult it can be to find a parking spot. It's packed with vehicles owned by people with good intentions, and armed with a NYR to lose weight and get in shape. However, if you go back to the gym closer to the end of the month, you'll notice that half of the parking lot is empty. Not armed with a proven strategy to stick with their new habits, the majority continue to fail.

Why is it so difficult to implement and sustain the habits we need to be happy, healthy and successful?

Addicted to the old: change is painful

Yes, we are, at some level, addicted to our habits. Whether psychologically or physically, once a habit has been reinforced through enough repetition, it can be very difficult to change. That is, if you don't have an effective, proven strategy.

One of the primary reasons most people fail to create and sustain new habits is because they don't know what to expect, and they don't have a winning strategy.

How long does it *really* take to form a new habit?

Depending on the article you read or which expert you listen to, you'll hear compelling evidence that it takes anywhere from a single hypnosis session, 21 days, or even up to three months to incorporate a new habit into your life – or get rid of an old one.

The popular 21-day myth may come from the 1960 book *Psycho-Cybernetics: A New Way To Get More Living Out of Life.*

Written by cosmetic surgeon Dr. Maxwell Maltz, he found that amputees took, on average, 21 days to adjust to the loss of a limb. He argued that people take 21 days to adjust to any major life changes. Some would argue that how long it takes for a habit to become truly automatic also depends on the difficulty of the habit.

My personal experience and the real-world results I've seen working with hundreds of coaching clients has led me to the conclusion that you can change any habit in 30 days, if you have the right strategy. The problem is, most people don't have any strategy, let alone the right one. So, year after year, they lose confidence in themselves and their ability to improve, as failed attempt after failed attempt piles up and knocks them down. Something has to change.

How can *you* become a master of your habits? How can you take complete control of your life – and your future – by learning how to identify, implement and sustain any positive habit you want, and permanently remove any negative habit? You're about to learn the *right* strategy, one most people know nothing about.

The Miracle Morning 30-Day 'Habit Mastery' Strategy (that actually works)

One of the biggest obstacles preventing most people from implementing and sustaining positive habits is that they don't have the right strategy. They don't know what to expect and aren't prepared to overcome the mental and emotional challenges that are part of the process of implementing any new habit.

We'll start by dividing the 30-day time frame necessary to implement a positive new habit (or get rid of an old, negative habit) into three ten-day phases. Each of these phases presents a different set of emotional challenges and mental roadblocks to sticking with the new habit. Since the average person is not aware of these challenges and roadblocks, when they face them, they give up because they don't know what to do to overcome them.

[Days 1–10] Phase One: *Unbearable*

The first ten days of implementing any new habit, or ridding yourself of any old habit, can *feel* almost unbearable. Although the first few days can be easy, and even exciting – because it's something *new* – as soon as the newness wears off, reality sets in. You hate it. It's painful. It's not fun anymore. Every fibre of your being tends to resist and reject the change. Your mind rejects it and you think: *I hate this.* Your body resists it and tells you: *I don't like how this feels.*

If your new habit is waking up early (which might be a useful one to get started on, now), during the first ten days your experience might be something like this: [The alarm clock sounds] *Oh God, it's morning already! I don't want to get up. I'm soooo tired. I need more sleep. Okay, just ten more minutes.* [Hit snooze button]

The problem for most people is that they don't realize that this seemingly unbearable first ten days is only 'temporary'. Instead, they think it's the way the new habit feels, and will always feel, telling themselves: *If the new habit is this painful, forget it – it's not worth it.*

As a result, 95% of our society – the mediocre majority – fail, time and time again, to start exercise routines, quit smoking, improve their diets, stick to a budget, or any other habit that would improve their quality of life.

Here's where you have an advantage over the other 95%. See, when you are *prepared* for these first ten days, when you know that it is the price you pay for success, that the first ten days will be challenging but they're also *temporary*, you can beat the odds and succeed! If the benefits are great enough, we can do anything for ten days, right?

So, the first ten days of implementing any new habit aren't a picnic. You'll defy it. You might even hate it at times. But *you can do it*. Especially considering, it only gets easier from here, and the reward is, oh – just the ability to create *everything* you want for your life.

[Days 11–20] Phase Two: *Uncomfortable*

After you get through the first ten days – the most difficult ten days – you begin the second ten-day phase, which is considerably easier. You will be getting used to your new habit. You will also have developed some confidence and positive associations to the benefits of your habit.

While days 11–20 are not unbearable, they are still uncomfortable and will require discipline and commitment on your part. At this stage it will still be tempting to fall back to your old behaviours. Referencing the example of *waking up early* as your new habit, it will still be easier to sleep in because you've done it for so long. Stay committed. You've already gone from *unbearable* to *uncomfortable*, and you're about to find out what it feels like to be *UNSTOPPABLE*.

[Days 21–30] Phase Three: *Unstoppable*

When you enter the final ten days – the home stretch – the few people that make it this far almost always make a detrimental mistake: adhering to the popular advice from the many experts who claim it only takes 21 days to form a new habit.

Those experts are partly correct. It does take 21 days – the first two phases – to *form* a new habit. But the third ten-day phase is crucial to sustaining your new habit, long term. The final ten days is where you positively reinforce and associate pleasure with your new habit. You've been primarily associating pain and discomfort with it during the first 20 days. Instead of hating and resisting your new habit, you start feeling proud of yourself for making it this far.

Phase Three is also where the actual *transformation* occurs, as your new habit becomes part of your *identity*. It transcends the space between *something you're trying* and *who you're becoming*. You start to see yourself as someone who lives the habit.

Back to our example of waking up early: you go from having an identity that says I am *not* a 'morning person' to *I am a morning person*! Instead of dreading your alarm clock in the morning, now when the alarm goes off you are excited to wake up and get going because you've done it for over 20 days in a row. You're starting to see and feel the benefits.

Too many people get overly confident, pat themselves on the back and think: *I've done it for 20 days so I'm just going to take a few days off.* The problem is that those first twenty days are the most challenging part of the process. Taking a few days off before you've invested the necessary time into positively reinforcing the habit makes it difficult to get back on. It's days 21–30 where you really start enjoying the habit, which is what will make you continue it in the future.

But I hate running

'I'm not a runner though, Jon. In fact, I hate running. There's no way I could do it.'

'Come on, Hal – it's to raise money for the Front Row Foundation,' Jon Berghoff responded. 'Look, I didn't think I could do a marathon either, but once you commit to it, you'll find a way to make it happen. And I'm telling you, it is truly a life-changing experience!'

'I'll think about it.'

Telling Jon I would *think* about it was really just my way of getting him off my back. Don't get me wrong, I absolutely believed in and supported the life-changing work done by the Front Row Foundation. I had been donating money to the organization for years, but writing a cheque was a little easier than running a marathon. Unless I was being chased, I hadn't intentionally run so much as a block in the ten years since I graduated high school. And even back then I only ran to keep from failing PE class.

Besides, ever since breaking my femur and pelvis in the car accident, back when I was 20, I was always afraid of what might happen if I put too much pressure on my leg. In fact, every time I went snow skiing, I couldn't help but have visions of me tripping and taking a hard fall, then having the metal rod in my leg break through the skin of my thigh. It's a gruesome thought, but breaking your limbs and being told you may never walk again can do that to you.

A week later after my conversation with Jon, one of my coaching clients – Katie Fingerhut – completed her second marathon. 'Hal, it's so amazing… I feel like I can do anything now!'

Between Jon and Katie's enthusiastic testimonies for marathon running, I was starting to think maybe it was time for me to overcome my limiting belief about *not being a runner*, and just start running. Like everything else in life, if they could do it, then so could I. So I did.

The next morning, intent on completing my first mile on my journey to completing a marathon, I put on my *basketball* shoes (sound familiar?) and headed out the front door of my house. I was actually looking forward to it! (Remember, the first few days of any *new* habit are often exciting.)

Down the driveway I hustled, motivated and inspired. Onto the sidewalk I ran. As I stepped from the sidewalk to the street, my ankle twisted on the curb and I collapsed. Lying on the pavement, writhing in pain and gripping my ankle, I thought to myself, *everything happens for a reason, so I guess today wasn't the day for me to start running… I'll try again tomorrow.* So I did.

30 Days: From unbearable to unstoppable"

That next day I officially began my marathon training. My excitement only lasted for a few blocks, as the physical pain began to remind me of what I believed for so long: *I am not a runner.* My hips ached. My femur was sore. But I was committed.

I completed my first painful mile, but I realized I needed help – I needed a plan. I drove to the bookstore and purchased the perfect book for me: *The Non-Runner's Marathon Trainer*, by David Whitsett. Now I had a plan.

- **Days 1–10:** The first ten days of running were both physically painful and mentally challenging. Every single day, I fought a constant battle in my head with the voice of mediocrity, telling me it was okay to quit. But it wasn't. *Do what's right, not what's easy*, I reminded myself. I kept running. I was committed.

- **Days 11–20:** Days 11–20 were only slightly less painful. I still didn't like running, but I didn't really hate it anymore. For the first time in my life, I was forming the habit of running every day. It was no longer this scary thing I only watched other people doing on the sidewalk while I was driving my car. After nearly two weeks of daily running, it was starting to feel normal for me to wake up every day, and just go for a run. I remained committed.

- **Days 21–30:** Days 21–30 were almost enjoyable. I had almost forgotten what it felt like to hate running. I was doing it without much thought. I just woke up, put on my running shoes (yes, I had invested in a pair), and logged my miles each day. The mental battle was gone, replaced with reciting positive affirmations or listening to self-improvement audios while I ran. In just 30 days, I had overcome my limiting belief that I couldn't run. I was becoming what I would have never imagined in a million years... I was becoming a runner.

The rest of the story: '52 miles To freedom'

Just 30 days after beginning the habit of running – something that had been so foreign and unpleasant to me for my entire life – I had completed 50 miles, culminating in my first six-mile run. I called Jon to celebrate. He was excited for me, and always looking to help me raise my own standards, he presented me with a challenge. Jon knew me well enough to know that in the peak emotional state I was in, I would likely accept any challenge. 'Hal, why don't you run an *ultra*-marathon? If you're going to run 26 miles, you might as well run 52.' Only Jon would suggest such logic.

'I'll think about it.'

This time, when I told Jon I would *think about it*, I actually meant it. I was intrigued by the idea of pushing myself even further and running 52 consecutive miles. Maybe Jon was right. If I was going to run 26, I might as well run 52. I mean, shoot, if I could go from running *zero* miles to being able to run six consecutive miles in just four weeks, and I still had six months until the Front Row Foundation's annual 'Run for the Front' charity run, why not set the bar a little higher and go for 52? So I did. I was even somehow able to convince a friend and two of my brave coaching clients to do it with me!

Six months later I had logged 475 miles, including three 20-mile runs, and had travelled across the country to meet with two of my favourite coaching clients James Hill and Favian Valencia, and long-time friend, Alicia Anderer, so the four of us could attempt to run 52 miles during the Atlantic City Marathon. Jon even flew out to show his support. There was just one logistical challenge though: Atlantic City wasn't set up for any 'ultra' marathon runners. So, we improvised.

We met on the Boardwalk at 3.30 am. Our goal was to finish our first 26 miles before the official marathon began, then complete the second half with the regular marathon runners.

The moment was surreal. The energy between the four of us was a blend of excitement, fear, adrenaline, and disbelief. Were we *really* going to do this?!

We might have been able to see our breath in the chill October air had the moonlight been brighter. Nevertheless, our path was well enough lit, and so we began. One foot in front of the other, one step at a time, we moved forward. We all agreed that was the key to our success that day – keep moving forward. So long as we didn't stop putting one foot in front of the other, as long as we kept moving forward, we would eventually reach our destination.

Six hours and five minutes later, largely due to the collective support and accountability of our group working together as one unit, we completed our first 26 miles. This was a defining moment for each of us. Not because of the 26 miles we had behind us, but because of the mental fortitude it was going to take to get ourselves to run the 26 miles we had ahead of us.

The excitement which permeated every fibre of our being just six hours earlier had been replaced with excruciating pain, fatigue and mental exhaustion. Considering the physical and mental state we were in, we just didn't know if we had it in us to duplicate what we had just done. But we did.

A total of 15½ hours from the time we started, James, Favian, Alicia and I completed our 52-mile quest… together. One foot in front of the other, and one step at a time, we ran, jogged, walked, limped, and literally crawled across the finish line.

On the other side of that line was *freedom* – the kind of freedom that can never be taken away from you. It was freedom from our self-imposed limitations. Although through our training we had grown to believe that running 52 consecutive miles was *possible*, none of us really believed in our heart of hearts that it was probable. As individuals, each of us struggled with our own fear and self-doubt. But the moment we crossed that finish line, we had given ourselves the gift of freedom from our fears, our self-doubt, and our self-imposed limitations.

It was in that moment I realized that this is a gift of freedom not reserved for the chosen few, but one that is available to each and every one of us the moment we make the choice to take on *challenges* that are out of our comfort zone, forcing us to grow, to expand our capacity, to be and do more than we have been and done in the past. This is true freedom.

Are you ready for true freedom?

The Miracle Morning 30-Day Life Transformation Challenge (in the next chapter) will enable you to overcome your own self-imposed limitations so you can be, do, and have everything you want in your life, faster than you ever thought possible. *The Miracle Morning* is a life-changing daily habit, and while most people who try it, love it from day one, getting yourself to follow through with it for 30 days – so you can make it a lifelong habit – will require an unwavering commitment from you.

On the other side of the next 30 days is you – becoming the person you need to be to create everything you've ever wanted for your life. Seriously, what could be more exciting than that?

10

The Miracle Morning 30-Day Life Transformation Challenge

An extraordinary life is all about daily, continuous improvements
in the areas that matter most.

Robin Sharma

Life begins at the end of your comfort zone.

Neale Donald Walsh

Let's play devil's advocate for a moment. Can *The Miracle Morning* really transform your life in just 30 days? I mean, come on – can anything really make *that* significant of an impact on your life, that quickly? Well, remember that it did for me, even when I was at my lowest point. It has for thousands of others. Ordinary people, just like you and me, becoming extraordinary.

In the last chapter you learned the simplest and most effective strategy for successfully implementing and sustaining any new habit in 30 days. During The *Miracle Morning 30-Day Life Transformation Challenge* you'll identify the habits you believe will have the most significant impact on your life, your success, who you want to be and where you want to go. Then, you'll use the next 30 days to form these habits, which will completely transform the *direction* of your life, your health, your wealth, your relationships and any other aspect that you choose. By changing the direction of your life, you immediately change your quality of life, and ultimately, where you end up.

Consider the rewards

When you commit to *The Miracle Morning 30-Day Life Transformation Challenge*, you will be building a foundation for success in every area of your life, for the rest of your life. By waking up each morning and practising *The Miracle Morning*, you will begin each day with extraordinary levels of *discipline* (the crucial ability to get yourself to follow through with your commitments), *clarity* (the power you'll generate from focusing on what's most important), and *personal development* (perhaps the single most significant determining factor in your success). Thus, in the next 30 days you'll find yourself quickly *becoming the person* you need to be to create the extraordinary levels of personal, professional, and financial success you truly desire.

You'll also be transforming *The Miracle Morning* from a concept that you may be excited (and possibly a little nervous) to 'try' into a lifelong habit, one that will continue to develop you into the person you need to be to create the life you've always wanted. You'll begin to fulfil your potential and see results in your life far beyond what you've ever experienced before.

In addition to developing successful habits, you'll also be developing the *mindset* you need to improve your life – both internally and externally. By practising the *Life S.A.V.E.R.S.* each day, you'll be experiencing the physical, intellectual, emotional, and spiritual benefits of *Silence, Affirmations, Visualization, Exercise, Reading,* and *Scribing.* You'll immediately feel less stressed, more centred, focused, happier and more excited about your life. You'll be generating more energy, clarity and motivation to move towards your highest goals and dreams (especially those you've been putting off far too long).

Remember, your life situation will improve after – but only *after* – you develop yourself into the person you need to be to improve it. That's exactly what these next 30 days of your life can be – a new beginning, and a new you.

You can do this!

If you're feeling hesitant, or concerned about whether or not you will be able to follow through with this for 30 days, relax – it's completely normal to feel that way. This is especially true if waking up in the morning is something you've found challenging in the past. Remember, we all suffer from RMS (rear-view mirror syndrome – see Chapter 10). So, it's not only expected that you would be a bit hesitant or nervous, but it's actually a sign that you're *ready* to commit, otherwise you wouldn't be nervous.

It is also important that you take confidence from the thousands of other people who have already gone from living on the wrong side of their *potential gap* to completely transforming their lives with *The Miracle Morning*. In fact, I'd like to take a moment to revisit and review a handful of the success stories that were shared in the opening pages of this book. I really believe the example of others can shine light on what's possible for us.

- I was so inspired by the transformation that Melanie Deppen, an entrepreneur from Selinsgrove, PA shared with us: 'I am on day 79 of *The Miracle Morning*, and since I began, I have not missed a single day. Honestly, this is the FIRST time in my life that I've ever set out to do something and have actually stuck with it for more than just a couple of days or weeks. I now look forward to waking up every day! It's incredible, *The Miracle Morning* has completely changed my life.'

- I couldn't help but wish I had known about *The Miracle Morning* in college, or even high school, after hearing the difference it made for Michael Reeves, a student from Walnut Creek, CA: 'When I first heard about *The Miracle Morning*, I thought to myself, "this is so crazy that it just might work!" I am a college student taking 19 units and working full time, so that left me with zero time to work on my goals. Before I learned about *The Miracle Morning*, I used to wake up between 7–9 am every day – because I had to get ready for class – but now I consistently wake up at 5 am. I am learning and growing so much through daily personal development, and I am LOVING *The Miracle Morning*!'

- Speaking of college students, Natanya Green – now a yoga instructor in Sacramento, CA – began fulfilling her potential with the help of *The Miracle Morning* while attending a California University: 'After beginning *The Miracle Morning* in December, 2009, as a college student at UC Davis, I noticed profound changes immediately. I quickly began to achieve long-desired goals more easily than I would have ever expected. I lost weight, found a new love, attained my best grades ever, and even created multiple streams of income – all in less than two months! Now, years later, *The Miracle Morning* is still an integral part of my daily life.'

- How could you not be impressed by the extraordinary level of commitment shown by Ray Ciafardini, a District Manager from Baltimore, MD: 'I'm on my 83rd consecutive day of *The Miracle Morning* and just wish I had known about it sooner. It is amazing how much clarity I have throughout the day, now, thanks to *The Miracle Morning*. I am able to focus on my work and all other tasks each day with so much more energy and enthusiasm. Thanks to *The Miracle Morning*, I am experiencing a richer, more abundant way of living – in both my personal and my professional life.'

- Finally, I was blown away by the powerful story from Rob Leroy, a Senior Account Executive in Sacramento, CA: 'A few months ago, I decided to try *The Miracle Morning*. My life is changing so fast I cannot keep up! I'm such a better person because of this – and it's infectious. My business was struggling, but after I started *The Miracle Morning* I was amazed at how, just by working on myself every day, I was able to turn it all around!"

These success stories are from normal, everyday people, just like you and me. People who were living below their potential and used *The Miracle Morning* to finally close the gap and achieve the success they truly want, and deserve. Now is a good time to be reminded of one of the most important success principles for you and I to live by: *If they can do it, so can we.*

3.1 Steps to begin *The Miracle Morning* (30-Day) Life Transformation Challenge

Step 1

Visit www.MiracleMorning.com/resources to download your free '*Miracle Morning 30-Day Life Transformation Challenge* Fast Start Kit' – complete with the exercises, affirmations, daily checklists, tracking sheets and everything else you need to make starting and completing *The Miracle Morning 30-Day Life Transformation Challenge* as easily as possible. Take a minute to do this now.

Step 2

Commit to and schedule your first Miracle Morning as soon as possible – ideally tomorrow (yes, actually write it into your schedule) – and decide where it will take place. Remember, it's recommended that you leave your bedroom and remove yourself from the temptations of your bed altogether. My Miracle Morning takes place every day on my living room couch while everyone else in my house is still sound asleep. I've heard from people who do their Miracle Morning sitting outside in nature, such as on their porch or deck, or at a nearby park. Do yours where you feel most comfortable, but also where you won't be interrupted.

Step 3

Read the introduction in your '*Miracle Morning 30-Day Life Transformation Challenge* Fast Start Kit', then follow the instructions, and complete the exercises. Like anything in life that's worthwhile, successfully completing *The Miracle Morning 30-Day Life Transformation Challenge* requires a bit of preparation. It's important that you do the initial exercises in your 'Fast Start Kit' (which shouldn't take you more than 30–60 minutes) and keep in mind that your Miracle Morning will always start with the *preparation* you do the day or night before to get yourself ready mentally, emotionally, and logistically for *The Miracle Morning.* This preparation includes the five-step snooze-proof wake-up strategy (Chapter 5).

Step 3.1
Get an accountability partner. In Chapter 3, we discussed the undeniable link between accountability and success. All of us benefit from the support that comes from embracing a higher level of accountability, so it's highly recommended – but not required – that you get a like-minded accountability partner to join you in *The Miracle Morning 30-Day Life Transformation Challenge.*

Not only does having someone to hold us accountable increase the odds that we will follow through, but joining forces with someone else is simply more fun! Consider that when you're excited about something and committed to doing it on your own, there is a certain level of power in that excitement and in your individual commitment. However, when you have someone else in your life – a friend, family member, or co-worker – and they're as excited about it and committed to it as you are, it's much more powerful.

Call, text, or email one or more people today, and invite them to join you for *The Miracle Morning 30-Day Life Transformation Challenge.* The quickest way to get them up to speed is to send them the link www.MiracleMorning.com so they can get free and immediate access to 'The Miracle Morning Crash Course' – two free chapters of *The Miracle Morning* book, *The Miracle Morning* video training and *The Miracle Morning* audio training.

It will cost them nothing, and you'll be teaming up with someone who is also committed to taking their life to the next level, so the two of you can support, encourage, and hold each other accountable.

IMPORTANT: Don't wait until you have an accountability partner on board to do your first Miracle Morning and start *The Miracle Morning 30-Day Life Transformation Challenge.* Whether or not you've found someone to embark on the journey with you, I recommend scheduling and doing your first Miracle Morning tomorrow – no matter what. Don't wait. You'll be even more capable of inspiring someone else to do *The Miracle Morning* with you if you've already experienced a few days of it. Get started. Then, as soon as you can, invite a friend, family member, or co-worker to visit www.MiracleMorning.com to get their free Miracle Morning crash course. In less than an hour, they'll be fully capable of being your Miracle Morning Accountability Partner – and probably a little inspired.

Are you ready to take your life to the next level?

What is the next level in your personal or professional life? Which areas need to be transformed in order for you to reach that level? Allow yourself the gift of investing just 30 days to make significant improvements in your life, one day at a time. No matter what your past has been, you *can* change your future, by changing the present.

Conclusion

*Let today be the day you give up who you've been
for who you can become*

Every day, think as you wake up, 'Today I am fortunate to have
woken up, I am alive, I have a precious human life, I am not
going to waste it. I am going to use all my energies to develop
myself, to expand my heart out to others. I am going to benefit
others as much as I can.'

Dalai Lama

Things do not change. We change.

Henry David Thoreau

Where you are is a result of who you *were*, but where you
end up depends entirely on who you choose to be from this
moment forward.

It's your time. Don't put off creating and experiencing the
life – happiness, health, wealth, success and love – that you truly
want and deserve for another day. As my mentor Kevin Bracy
always urged: 'Don't wait to be great.' If you want your life to
improve, you have to improve yourself first. Get '*The Miracle
Morning 30-Day Life Transformation* Fast Start Kit' today at
www.MiracleMorning.com/resources. Then, with or without
an accountability partner, commit to your first Miracle Morning
and beginning your *30-Day Life Transformation Challenge* tomorrow. You know, *tomorrow* – the day you begin your journey to
creating the most extraordinary life you have ever imagined.

If there is anything I can do to support you or add value to your life in any way, please let me know.

Contact me – any time

I'm always grateful to connect with like-minded folks, and find it especially cool to hear from people who have read my books, seen my videos, or attended my speeches. So, if you have any questions or would just like to say hi, go to www.YoPalHal.com and click on the 'Contact' tab to send me a message. I look forward to hearing from you, and exploring how I can add as much value to your life as I possibly can.

Let's keep helping others

May I ask you a quick favour?

If this book has added value to your life, if you feel like you're better off after reading it, and you see that *The Miracle Morning* can be a new beginning for you to take any – or every – area of your life to the next level, I'm hoping you'll do something for someone you love: give this book to them. Let them borrow your copy. Ask them to read it. Or better yet, get them their own copy, maybe as a birthday or Christmas gift. Come to think of it – what better book to give someone for Christmas than the only book that *makes every morning feel like Christmas?!*

Or it could be for no special occasion at all, other than to say, 'Hey, I love and appreciate you, and I want to help you live your best life. Read this.'

If you believe, as I do, that being a great friend or family member is about helping your friends and loved ones to become the best versions of themselves, I encourage you to share this book with them.

Please spread the word. Thank you so much.

A special invitation
(in case you missed it the first time!)

The Miracle Morning Community

Fans and readers of *The Miracle Morning* make up an extraordinary tribe of like-minded individuals, who wake up each day *on purpose*, dedicated to fulfilling the unlimited potential that is within each of us. As creator of *The Miracle Morning*, I felt it was my responsibility to create an online community where readers and fans could go to connect, get encouragement, share best practices, support one another, discuss the book, post videos, find an accountability partner, and even swap smoothie recipes and exercise routines.

I honestly had no idea that *The Miracle Morning* Community would become one of the most positive, inspired, supportive and accountable online communities that I have ever seen, but it has. I'm truly blown away by the calibre of our members.

Just go to www.MiracleMorning.com/resources and request to join *The Miracle Morning* Community on Facebook. Here you'll be able to connect with like-minded individuals who are already practising *The Miracle Morning* – many of whom have been doing it for years – to get additional support and accelerate your success.

I'll be moderating the community and checking in regularly. I look forward to seeing you there!

If you'd like to connect with me personally on social media, follow @HalElrod on Twitter and www.Facebook.com/YoPal-Hal on Facebook. Please feel free to send me a direct message, leave a comment, or ask me a question. I do my best to answer every single one, so let's connect soon!

An essential bonus

The email that will change your life

Everybody needs feedback, and it's a heck of a lot cheaper
than paying a trainer.

Doug Lowenstein

Ask for feedback from people with diverse backgrounds.
Each one will tell you one useful thing.

Steve Jobs

It was 2 o'clock in the morning. I couldn't sleep. Still renting a room from Matt, I was sitting at my cheap imitation-pine desk, crammed into my 12' × 12' living space. This sucked. Something had to change. Or maybe *I* needed to change.

Staring at my laptop and feeling frustrated with my life, I suddenly got inspired. I don't remember exactly what prompted it, but I opened up a new email and started adding a very diverse group of people to the *To:* field. Close friends, family, coworkers, former bosses, acquaintances, the girl I was dating, and even – believe it or not – my ex-girlfriends. You name it, I was ready to make some radical changes in my life. I was ready for a quantum leap in my potential, and I felt the only way for me to get an accurate assessment of who I was, how I was showing up in my life, and where I needed to improve was to solicit honest feedback from the people who knew me best.

I stopped when I got to 23 email addresses, because, well, I am a huge fan of Michael Jordan and have a mild obsession with the number 23. I began to compose an email to these people, who each knew me in different capacities and to varying degrees, explaining that I wanted to grow personally, to be a better friend, son, brother, and colleague, and that the only thing to do was to get feedback from people who could see things about me that I couldn't see about myself. I asked if they would please take a few minutes to reply, at their earliest convenience, sharing what they believed were the three biggest areas that I needed to improve. I asked that they be brutally honest, and assured them that they would not hurt my feelings. In fact, the only thing that would hurt my feelings was for them to hold back, because doing so would only limit my growth.

I'd be lying if I didn't admit that this was the most nerve-racking email I've ever composed. I almost chickened out. I considered deleting it, and just going to bed. Thank God I didn't. No, I took a deep breath, and I clicked *send.* Then, I went to bed, fell asleep, and awaited their responses.

Six hours later, I woke up. Wait, *did I really send that email at 2 o'clock in the morning, or was that just a dream*? I logged into my email. Nope, not a dream. I definitely sent it. And I already had two replies. One was from my mother, and the other was from J. Brad Britton, a well-respected region manager at the $200 million company I worked for. *Oh boy, here goes…* I paused for a second and reminded myself that the purpose of this exercise was for me to grow and improve, so no matter what anyone said in his or her email, I was going to keep an open mind and not get offended. Easier said than done.

I opened my mom's email first. *Hey son, I got your email.* (Really Mom? I had no idea that you got it.) *Well, you know I think you're perfect! But if I must give you some constructive feedback, it's that you should call your mother more often! I know you're busy, but it would be nice to hear from you every once in a while. Anyway, I love you! Come visit soon … Love, Mom.* I opened up a blank document on my computer and titled it 'Constructive feedback and my new commitments #1: Call Mom at least once a week.'

Then I opened the email from my Region Manager, J. Brad Britton. J. Brad is someone I admired and had learned a great deal from. Not to mention, he was one of the most positive people I knew. Although we only saw each other a few times throughout the year at conferences and on company trips, he knew me well, at least in a professional capacity. *My Pal Hal! I love your email. However, I am only willing to give you the three pieces of constructive feedback you have requested if you let me follow it up with three things I like about you. Deal? Okay, here goes…*

J. Brad proceeded to enlighten me to a few of my professional and social 'blind spots', all of which caught me by surprise. To be honest, my feelings did get a bit hurt. I felt a little defensive. *That's not true. I'm not really like that. He obviously doesn't know me as well as I thought he did.* Then, it occurred to me that it didn't matter how accurate each of his criticisms were, because that was how I was showing up for him – and probably many others. It was important to me not just that *I* knew who I *really was*, but that I was living in alignment with my values, and congruent in all of my relationships.

Email responses continued to pour in over the next few days. By the end of the week, 17 of the 23 recipients had replied with their thoughtful and (mostly) constructive criticisms. I had added a lot to my 'Constructive feedback and my new commitments' document since making a note of my mom's request for more frequent contact. So, what were the results?

Let's just say that I gained more *self-awareness* and grew more in a week from reading those responses than I had grown in the previous five years combined – and possibly my entire life. It was incredible. It wasn't easy to put myself in such a vulnerable position and look at all of my flaws – but it *was* life-changing. It was career-advancing. It was relationship-improving. And it was all a result of mustering up enough courage to send what is probably the most important email that I have ever sent: *the email that will change your life*.

Before I give you *the email that will change your life* below, word-for-word – so you can copy, edit, and send it to your circle of influence – I'd like to take a moment to share some positive feedback with you from one of my coaching clients. She sent this to me after she had sent *the email that will change your life* to her circle of influence:

From Trudy, one of my VIP Success Coaching clients:

Hal, I can't believe how effective that email you gave us, the one for requesting personal feedback, has been for me so far. Every reply I've received addresses my weaknesses and strengths from the different respective angles of my friends, co-workers, and family members that know me. This has presented me with a more complete picture of myself, and I feel so respected to receive the help from everyone. Not to mention, the email is also found unique and was well-received by everyone who received it!

Thank you, Hal, for helping me so much with your VIP Success Coaching.
With gratefulness, Trudy

The email that will change your life

Problem: Feedback avoidance. Most people don't enjoy negative feedback, so they completely avoid asking for feedback. This prevents them from gaining invaluable data about their strengths and weaknesses, thus preventing them from capitalizing on the former and significantly improving the latter.

Solution: Actively seeking and learning from the honest feedback of people who know you (in various capacities) is one of the *most effective* and *fastest* ways to gain a new perspective and accelerate your personal development and success.

Instructions: Type the following text into an email (feel free to edit and personalize the email so that it sounds like you.) Send it to between five and thirty people (the more the better) who know you well enough to give you an honest assessment of your strengths and weaknesses. This may include friends, family, colleagues, mentors, teachers, former employers or managers, customers, your significant other, and if you're brave enough... wait for it – your ex-significant others. (Seriously.)

Important: Be sure to put the outgoing email addresses in the BCC field of the email, so that each recipient doesn't see everyone else you're sending it to. (Or, you can copy and paste, then send the email to each person individually.)

Subject line: *This means a lot... Or Would love to get your opinion...*

Email Text:

Dear friends, family, and colleagues.

Thank you so much for reading this email. This isn't an easy one for me to send, but it is extremely important to me, so I sincerely appreciate you investing your valuable time reading (and hopefully responding to) it.

This email is going out to only a select group of people. Each of you knows me well, and I'm hoping will give me honest feedback about my strengths and most importantly, my weaknesses (aka 'areas of improvement'.)

I've never done anything like this before, but I feel that for me grow and improve as a person, I need to get a more accurate picture of how I'm showing up to the people that matter most to me. In order to become the person I need to be to create the life and contribute to others at the levels that I want, I need your feedback.

So, all I'm asking is that you take just a few minutes to email me back with what you honestly think are my top two/three 'areas of improvement'. If it will make you feel better to also list my top two/three 'strengths' (I'm sure it will make me feel better), you are definitely welcome to. That's it. And please don't sugarcoat it or hold back anything. I will not be offended by anything that you share. In fact, the more 'brutally' honest you are, the more leverage it will give me to make positive changes in my life.

Thank you again, and if there is anything else I can do to add value to your life, please let me know.

With sincere gratitude,

[Your name]

Final thoughts on the email that will change your life

That's it! I hope you will join me, Trudy, and my hundreds of other VIP Success Coaching clients (VIPSuccessCoaching.

com) who have mustered up the courage to be vulnerable and send this email. Some of the life-changing rewards you can count on will be increased self-awareness, deeper understanding of yourself, and clarity on the changes you can make to quickly take yourself and your life to the next level.

With sincere gratitude,

Yo Pal Hal

Thought-provoking quotes

I believe that a single idea can change the way we think, the way we feel, and the way we live. Thought-provoking quotes are one of my favourite means of encapsulating powerful, life-changing ideas. So, I have a passion for creating quotes that can inspire, empower, and challenge YOU to be better than you've ever been before.

Here are some of my favourite and most popular quotes. If any resonate with you, you might consider adding them to your affirmations, sharing them on Facebook or Twitter, set them as your computer desktop, put them on a T-shirt, have them tattooed on your lower back, or whatever floats your boat...

Love the life you have *while* you create the life of your dreams.
Don't think you have to wait for the latter to start doing
the former.

Where you are is a result of who you were, but where you go
depends entirely on who you choose to be.

Give up the need to be perfect for the opportunity to be
authentic. Be who you are. Love who you are. Others will too.

Replace your judgments with empathy, upgrade your
complaining to gratitude, and trade in your fear for love.

Be grateful for all that you have, accept all that you don't, and
actively create all that you want.

Life isn't about wishing you were somewhere or someone that
you're not. Life is about enjoying where you are, loving who you
are, and consistently improving both.

They say misery loves company, but so does mediocrity. Don't let the limiting beliefs of OTHERS limit what's possible for YOU.

Don't worry about trying to impress people. Just focus on how you can add value to their lives.

The moment you accept responsibility for EVERYTHING in your life is the moment you tap into your power to change ANYTHING in your life.

Every single one of us already has everything we need to be the happiest we could ever be; it's simply up to us to remember that in every moment.

There is nothing to fear, because you cannot fail. Only LEARN, GROW, and become BETTER than you've ever been before.

Know that wherever you are in your life right now is both temporary and exactly where you're supposed to be. You have arrived at this moment to learn what you must learn so that you can become the person you need to be to create everything you've ever wanted for your life.

Even when life is difficult or challenging – *especially* when life is difficult and challenging – the present is always an opportunity for us to learn, grow, and become better than we've ever been before.

Who you're becoming is far more important than what you're doing. And yet, it is what you're doing that is determining who you're becoming.

Your entire life changes the day that you decide you will no longer accept mediocrity for yourself. When you decide that today is the most important day of your life, and that now matters more than any other time because it's who you're becoming each day based on the choices you're making and the actions you're taking, that is determining who you are going to be for the rest of your life.

The average person lets their emotions dictate their actions, while achievers let their commitments dictate their actions.

Make bold moves toward your dreams each day, refuse to stop, and nothing can stop you.

Further reading

Chapman, G.D. *The Five Love Languages* (Moody Press, 2015)

DeMarco, M.J. *The Millionaire Fastlane* (Viperion Publishing, 2011)

Dunn, J. *The SoulMate Experience* (A Higher Possibility, first edition, 2011)

Goldsmith, M. *What Got You Here Won't Get You There: How Successful People become even more successful* (Profile Books, 2008)

Gottman, J.M. *The Seven Principles For Making a Marriage Work* (Orion, 2007)

Harv Eker, T. *Secrets of the Millionaire Mind* (Piatkus, 2007)

Hill, N., *Think and Grow Rich* (Wilder Publications, 2007)

Kelly, M. *The Rhythm of Life* (Simon & Schuster, 2006)

Pavlina, S., *Personal Development for Smart People* (Hay House, 2009)

Ramsey, D. *Total Money Makeover* (Thomas Nelson Publishers, reprint edition, 2013)

Stevenson, S. *Sleep Smarter: 21 Proven Tips to Sleep Your Way to a Better Body, Better Health, and Bigger Success.* (Model House Publishing, 2014)

Tracy, B. *Eat That Frog!* (Berrett-Koehler Publishers, 2007)

Whitsett, D. *The Non-Runner's Marathon Trainer* (McGraw Hill, 1998).

Williamson, M. *A Return To Love* (Thorsons, 1996)

Acknowledgements

Make sure you at least read the last paragraph (it's to YOU).

This may be the most challenging part of writing a book. Not because I am short on people to acknowledge – quite the opposite. There are so many people who have touched my life and made a significant impact that it would simply be impossible to thank them all in the next few pages. In fact, doing so could probably take up an entire book itself. The sequel to this book could be titled: *The Miracle Morning: Acknowledgements*. I don't know that too many people would buy it, but I would definitely enjoy writing it.

First, I have to give deep thanks to the woman who carried me around for 9½ months and gave me the *miracle of life* – Mom. I love you so much. Thank you for always believing in me, and disciplining me when I needed it. I still need it. Oh, and *you* need to come visit more often!

Dad, of all my best friends, you are my *best* friend. I am the man I am today because of the father you have been for me my entire life. You have instilled so many values and qualities in me, which I am even more grateful for now that I know I will be passing them on to my children. I love you, Dad.

To Hayley, you're the best sister ever. Hands down. No competition. However, not only are you a great sister, you truly are one of my best friends. You are authentic, supportive, kind, and you're *almost* as funny as I am! Seriously, I am so grateful that YOU are my sister – I couldn't imagine a better one.

To the real-life woman of my dreams – Ursula. You are everything that I have ever wanted in a wife, and so many things I never knew I needed, but now could never live without. I still marvel at how perfect you are *for me*, and I couldn't be more grateful to be creating and sharing our lives together. And how 'bout them cute kids we made, huh? Thank you for blessing me with Sophie and Halsten. With you at the helm, I know our family is destined for a lifetime of love and happiness.

To Sophie and Halsten, I know you can't read this yet, but I love you both so much. Thank you for each being everything I ever wanted in a child. I couldn't be more grateful for the joy and happiness that you bring to my life every day.

To my aunts, uncles, cousins and grandparents, I am so thankful for the immeasurable amount of love that you have always shown me. I love you all and I will always cherish the times we've shared together. I look forward to many more!

To my in-laws – Marek, Maryla, Steve, Linda, Adam and Ania – I am grateful to be a part of your family.

To my best friends – my *circle of influence* – any guy would be lucky to have any one of you in his life, and I somehow ended up with ALL of you! We've shared A LOT of great times together, but beyond that, it is *who you are* that makes me strive to be better. If it is true that we are the average of the five people we spend the most time with, I've got nothing to worry about! For your lifelong friendship, I love you: Jeremy Katen, Jon Berghoff, Matt Recore, Jon Vroman, Jesse Levine, Brad Weimert, Ruth Fields, John Ruhlin, Peter Voogd, Tony Carlston, Teddy Watson, Larry Rodriguez, Alex Hayden and Brian Bedel. To my many friends that I may not have mentioned here, know that it's not because I don't love you. I do.

To my extended family at Cutco and Vector – I can't thank you enough for the incredible opportunity you work so hard to provide for people, every day. To the Presidents, Bruce Goodman, Al DiLeonardo, and John Whelpley, and Executive VP,

Amar Davé – I think it's safe to say that each person I thank from this point forward is able to make the impact they do largely because of your leadership. Thank you for your extraordinary influence and the impact you have made in my life. To the Region Leaders – Jeff Bry, Earl Kelly, Scott Dennis, P.J. Potter, Loyd Reagan, and Mike Muriel, as well as the Division Managers, thank you for helping to shape my character, and continuing to give me opportunities to positively impact your people.

To my friends on the Cutco and Vector Executive teams: Jeff Kunkel, Fred Glaeser, John Kane, Steve Pokrzyk, Trent Booth, Adam Jester and Scott Gorrell – your selfless efforts positively impact the lives of thousands of people, including my own. I sincerely appreciate each of you. I would also like to thank the Stitt family for providing the foundation for all that is great about Cutco.

Thank you to the leaders and my friends at Vector Canada – Joe Cardillo, Angie MacDougall, Rhancha Connell, Sherrie Dickie, Michael Smith and Mike McDonald. Joe and Angie, it's been years since the first time you invited me to speak at one of your conferences, and I remember being so excited that I could finally officially call myself an 'international' speaker! You are always so generous, and I hope the trend of speaking at your events continues for many years to come.

Thank you to my writing and editing gurus – Joel D and Sue Canfield. You were the catalyst that finally got me writing again. This book wouldn't exist if it weren't for your expertise and accountability.

To my brilliant friend and the creator of BookMama.com, Linda Sivertsen – you are so talented and have such a gift for making any author's book idea into a bestselling masterpiece. Thank you for contributing your gifts to this book.

To Gail Lynne Goodwin, Ambassador of Inspiration at InspireMeToday.com. You are simply one of the nicest, most generous and inspiring people I have ever met. I'm grateful to have you in my life, and I can't wait to go sailing with you.

To the mentors, teachers, and authors who continue to lead through your example of courage and selflessness, and from whom I've learned so much: Robin Sharma, Brendon Burchard, Tony Robbins, Dave Durand, Tim Ferris, Matthew Kelly, Rudy Ruettiger, Anthony 'AB' Burke, Jeff Sooey, Wayne Dyer, Bill and Steve Harris, James Malinchak, Stephanie Chandler, Roger Crawford, Kevin Bracy, Will Bowen, John Maxwell, T. Harv Eker, Eckart Tolle, Dave Ramsey, Andrew Cohen, Ken Wilber, Seth Godin, Derek Sivers, Chris Brogan, Jonathan Sprinkles, Jonathan Budd and Michael Ellsberg.

To Kevin Bracy, you deserve significant credit. I was sitting in your seminar just days before my first Miracle Morning, and your words were the catalyst for me to overcome my limiting belief that I was *not* a 'morning person'. You reminded me, 'If you want your life to be different, you have to be willing to do something different, first'. I may have never attempted to wake up at 5 am – let alone written this book – if it weren't for you. Thank you.

To James Malinchak, you also deserve significant credit here. When I shared *The Miracle Morning* with you for the first time, you got excited, and you expanded my vision: 'Hal, I don't think you even see how big this is going to be, and how many people this is going to impact!' You have personally inspired tens of thousands of authors, speakers, and coaches to believe in their message, see it bigger, and impact more people. You did that for me, and I can't thank you enough.

To J. Brad Britton, you taught me one of the most valuable lessons, which I continue to live my life by and share with anyone who will listen – *do the right thing, not the easy thing*. You don't just teach it; you live it.

To Adam Stock, thank you for always adding value and wisdom to my life. Your profitability coaching has been invaluable!

To my assistant, Linda: you work so hard to ensure that our clients are well taken care of. Thank you so much for all that you do, and all of the value that you add to my life and to my family.

To the students, teachers, counsellors and advisers at every college or high school that I have ever spoken at: thank you for allowing me the opportunity to live my purpose through adding value to your lives.

To my private and VIP Success Coaching clients: I consider it a great privilege to be your Coach, and I thank you for allowing me to support you in achieving your goals and constantly becoming better versions of yourselves. Whether or not you realize it, I learn as much from you as you do from me. Again, thank you for allowing me to be your Coach.

To everyone who supported the launch of this book, your selflessness and commitment to paying forward the benefits you've received from *The Miracle Morning* have left me speechless. First, I have to thank TMM Launch Team – what a blast it was working with you to promote this book. I will forever be grateful and indebted to you. Special thanks to Kyle Smith, Isaac Stegman, Geri Azinger, Marc Ensign, Colleen Elliot Linder, Dashama, Mark Hartley, Dave Powders, Jon Berghoff, Jon Vroman, Jeremy Katen, Ryan Whiten, Robert Gonzalez, Carey Smolenski, Ryan Casey and Greg Strine.

Finally, to you, the reader: thank you for allowing me to be a part of your life. Let's keep connecting on Facebook, Twitter, and through *The Miracle Morning* Community. Please let me know how you're doing, and if there is ever anything I can do to add value to your life or support a cause you believe in, please don't hesitate to let me know. All right, now stop reading and start creating. Never settle. Create the life you deserve to live, and help others to do the same.

About the author

Hal Elrod is living proof that every single one of us has the ability to overcome our adversity and create the most extraordinary life we can imagine. At age 20, Hal was hit head-on by a drunk driver, died for six minutes, broke 11 bones, suffered permanent brain damage, and was told he would never walk again. Defying the logic of doctors and the temptations to be a victim, he has gone on to become a Hall of Fame business achiever, ultra-marathon runner, multiple-time #1 best-selling author, hip-hop recording artist, husband, father, and international keynote/motivational speaker.

Hal has dedicated his life to showing others how to overcome their challenges so that they can fulfil the unlimited potential that is within each of us. His other #1 best-selling book, *Taking Life Head On: How To Love the Life You Have While You Create the Life of Your Dreams* – is one of the highest rated and most acclaimed books on Amazon.com. (Read a few of the reviews, and you'll see why.)

Hal is also one of the top-rated keynote and motivational speakers in the US. While corporations and non-profits regularly bring Hal in to speak at their conferences and fundraisers, he has a passion for positively impacting young people. For more than a decade, 'Yo Pal' Hal's presentations have impacted over 100,000 audience members throughout the United States and Canada, with approximately 60,000 of those individuals having been high school and college students.

He has appeared on dozens of radio and television shows across the US, and he's been featured in numerous books, including *The Education of Millionaires, Cutting Edge Sales, Living College Life in the Front Row, The Author's Guide To Building An Online Platform, The 800-Pound Gorilla of Sales* and the bestselling *Chicken Soup for the Soul* series.

To contact Hal about media appearances, speaking at your event or on your campus, or if you just want to receive free training videos and resources, visit www.YoPalHal.com.

To connect with Hal on Twitter, follow @HalElrod, on Facebook at www.Facebook.com/YoPalHal, and through *The Miracle Morning* Community at www.MiracleMorning.com/resources.

Book Hal to speak

Book Hal to speak at your event and he's guaranteed to deliver an incredibly INSPIRING, highly ENTERTAINING and truly LIFE-CHANGING experience for everyone in attendance!

For more than a decade, Hal Elrod has been consistently rated as the #1 keynote speaker by meeting planners and attendees. His unique style combines *inspiring* audiences with his unbelievable TRUE story, keeping them laughing hysterically with his high energy, stand-up comedy style delivery, and *empowering* them with actionable strategies to take their RESULTS to the next level.

> As our keynote speaker, Hal received a standing ovation and was rated the #1 speaker out of 30+ presenters on our agenda.
>
> *Cutco Cutlery*

> Hal was the featured keynote speaker for 400 of our top sales performers and executives. He gave us a plan that was so simple, we had no choice but to put it into action immediately.
>
> *Art Van Furniture*

> Bringing Hal in to be the keynote speaker at our annual conference was the best investment we could have made.
>
> *Fidelity National Title*

For more information visit www.HalElrod.com